Journal Of My Life During The French Revolution

Grace Dalrymple Elliott

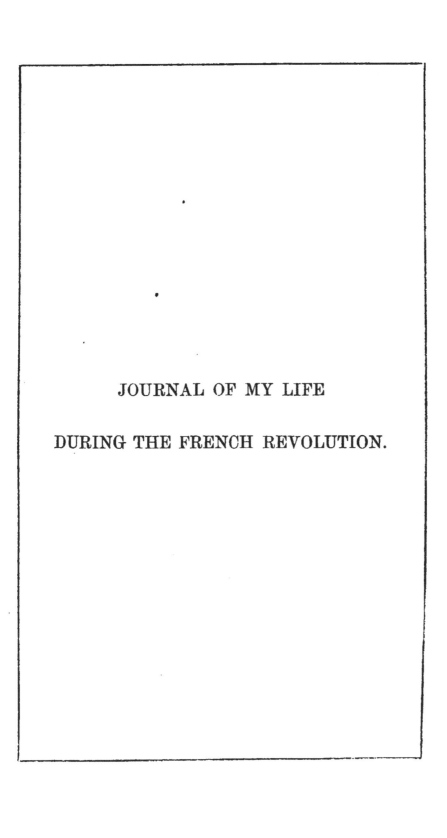

JOURNAL OF MY LIFE

DURING THE FRENCH REVOLUTION.

LONDON: PRINTED BY W. CLOWES AND SONS, STAMFORD-STREET.

Cosway. Pinx.   J. Brown. sc.

GRACE DALRYMPLE ELLIOTT.

JOURNAL

OF MY LIFE DURING

THE FRENCH REVOLUTION.

BY GRACE DALRYMPLE ELLIOTT.

LONDON:

RICHARD BENTLEY, NEW BURLINGTON STREET.

1859.

CONTENTS.

CHAPTER III.

CHAPTER IV.

CHAPTER V.

CHAPTER VI.

CHAPTER VII.

CONTENTS.

CHAPTER VIII.

PREFACE.

The following narrative of the Life of Mrs.
Dalrymple Elliott, during some of the most
eventful scenes of the great French Revolution,
was composed at the express desire of his
Majesty King George the Third. Mr. (afterwards Sir David) Dundas, physician to the king,
was also Mrs. Elliott's medical attendant; and
was in the habit of relating, during his visits
to the Royal Family, some of the incidents
and anecdotes which that lady had communi-
cated to him at various times, in the course
of conversation. The King became so much
interested that he desired Mr. Dundas to re-
quest Mrs. Elliott to commit to paper the story

of her Life in Paris, and to send it to him.
With this intimation she readily complied, and
accordingly the narrative was conveyed by Mr.
Dundas to Windsor, sheet by sheet as it was
written by her during her residence at Twick-
enham, after her return from France, at the
Peace of Amiens, in 1801.

Of her previous history Mrs. Dalrymple
Elliott has left no record; but the Editor has
gleaned a few facts relative to her birth and
earlier years from those who knew her intimately during her residence in England, at
the period when she drew up the following
narrative, which may be interesting to the
reader. She is represented as a lady eminently
gifted by nature with beauty of person, and
grace and elegance of manners; and she was
wont to attract the admiration of all who
approached her, while she conciliated the
regard and affection of those who were more
intimately acquainted with her.

Grace Dalrymple, the youngest of three daughters of Hew Dalrymple, Esq., a branch of, and next in succession to, the noble family of Stair, was born in Scotland, about 1765. Her father, a barrister, established his reputation by gaining for the plaintiff the celebrated Douglas and Hamilton cause, which Horace Walpole notices as one of the most remarkable of that period. He was afterwards appointed Attorney-General to the Grenadas. He deserted his wife, a woman of remarkable beauty, a daughter of an officer in the army, who returned to her father's house, which she never afterwards quitted, and where she gave birth to this her youngest daughter, Grace Dalrymple. This child was afterwards sent for her education to a convent in France, where she remained for some years, being withdrawn when she was about the age of fifteen, and brought to her father's house. At that time it was not the custom, as in these later days, for young persons to mix in evening festivities; but at one of the suppers given at her father's house, Miss Dalrymple was introduced. On this occasion, Sir John Elliott was present, a man older than her father; who was so struck with her beauty that he made her an offer of marriage, which was accepted by her with the same inconsiderate haste with which it was proffered. Such an unsuitable and ill-assorted marriage, as might naturally be supposed, was productive of nothing but unhappiness. There was such a total dissimilarity of tastes, as well as of age, that there never existed any affection between them.

Grace Dalrymple, now Mrs. Elliott, mixed much in general society; and being so exquisitely lovely, very soon found admirers amongst those more suited to her age. In an evil hour for her, she unhappily became entangled in an intrigue; and her husband, after some indecent treatment, resorted to a court of law at once to procure a divorce, and to punish the author of their mutual wrongs.

The first object was easily obtained, while the second resulted in a verdict of 12,000*l.* damages. In the mean time her brother removed her to a convent in France, assigning as a reason for the course which had been adopted, that the lady was about to contract an unsuitable marriage.

Here Mrs. Elliott remained until she was brought over to England by Lord Cholmondeley. She was subsequently introduced to the Prince of Wales, who had been struck with the exquisite beauty of her portrait, which he had accidentally seen at Houghton. So celebrated was she for her personal charms that there are several portraits of her by eminent painters still in existence, among others, one by Cosway, which embellishes this volume, another, by Gainsborough, at Lord Cholmondeley's.

The young Prince was immediately fascinated with her beauty, and a most intimate connexion succeeded. The result was the birth of a female child, who was christened at Marylebone church, under the names of Georgiana Augusta Frederica Seymour,—Lord Cholmondeley and one or two other persons only being present. While Mrs. Elliott remained with the Prince, she of course mingled in the brilliant society about him, and among many other persons of distinction became acquainted with the ill-fated Duke of Orleans, afterwards known as Philippe Egalité, so often mentioned in her memoirs. His fondness for England, its people, and its institutions was well known, and at that time he was popular here, especially in sporting society.

We cannot ascertain with certainty when Mrs. Elliott again left England to reside in Paris; but probably it was about the year 1786. Her little daughter was left in charge of Lord and Lady Cholmondeley, but was occasionally permitted to visit her mother at Paris. On these occasions she was always accompanied by a nurse and a footman of Lord Cholmondeley's; but she never resided any length of time with her mother. The Prince of Wales, it is said, made Mrs. Elliott a handsome allowance, and she derived 200*l.* a year also from her husband's family. With these few prefatory remarks we now leave her to tell her own interesting story.

MY LIFE

DURING

THE FRENCH REVOLUTION.

CHAPTER I.

OUTBREAK OF THE REVOLUTION.

IN the year 1789, July the 12th, which was
on a Sunday, I went, with the Duke of Orleans,
Prince Louis D'Aremberg, and others whose
names I do not recollect, to fish and dine at the
Duke's château of Raincy, in the Forest of
Bondy, near Paris. We returned to Paris in
the evening, meaning to go to the *Comédie
Italienne*. We had left Paris at eleven o'clock in
perfect tranquillity ; but on our return at eight
o'clock at the Porte St. Martin (where the
Duke's town-carriage was waiting for him, and
my carriage for me), my servant told me that

c

I could not go to the play, as the theatres were all shut by orders from the police; that Paris was all in confusion and tumult; that the Prince de Lambesc had entered the gardens of the Tuileries, and put all the people to flight; that he had killed an old man [not true]; that the French Guards and the regiment Royal Allemagne (which was the Prince of Lambesc's own regiment), were at that moment fighting on the Boulevards of the Chaussée D'Antin, opposite the depôt of the French Guards; that many cavaliers and horses had been killed; and that the mob were carrying about the streets the busts of the Duke of Orleans and of Necker, crying, " *Vive le Duc d' Orléans! Vive Necker!* "

When my servant had given me this information, I begged the Duke not to go into Paris in his own carriage, as I thought it would be very imprudent for him to appear in the streets at such a moment; and I offered him my carriage. On hearing of the events in Paris he seemed much surprised and shocked; he told me that he hoped it would be nothing, and that my servant, through fear, must have exaggerated the events. I thought that the Duke meant to show himself to the mob, and really had projects to make a party had he done so, but I never saw more unfeigned surprise than his when he heard that Paris was in such a situation. He then got into my carriage, and begged me to set him down at the *Salon des Princes*, a club frequented by all the nobility, and where he said he should meet people who would tell him the news. When we got to the club, however, it was also shut by a police order, as was every other club in Paris. We then ordered my coachman to drive to the Duke's house at Monceau, but as the troops were actually at that moment fighting on the Boulevards, and the ground was covered with dead and wounded men and horses, we were obliged to go by the Carrousel, and along the Tuileries garden-wall to the Place Louis Quinze, which we found full of troops, both horse and foot. They were commanded by the Mareschal de Broglie, and had been for some days before encamped in the Park of St. Cloud, and had marched into Paris that evening.

I never in my life shall forget the awful but beautiful appearance the Place Louis Quinze presented at that moment. The troops were under arms, and the silence was so great that if a pin had fallen it might have been heard. They allowed no carriages to pass without the name of the person being given. I gave *mine*, and my horses were conducted through the ranks of cavalry at a foot's pace. They had no idea that the Duke of Orleans was in my carriage. We went directly to the Duke's house at Monceau. By this time it was about a quarter past nine o'clock.

On the Duke's arrival he found his servants in the greatest confusion and uneasiness, as nobody knew at the Palais Royal where he was gone; and a report had been circulated in Paris that day that he had been put into the Bastille, and beheaded by the King's orders. They told him that all his friends and the Princes of the Blood had been at the Palais Royal and at Monceau to inquire about him; and that they were in the greatest consternation and anxiety. He, however, ordered his Suisse

to let nobody see him that night except the
Duc de Biron ; that he would sleep at Monceau,
but that if Madame de Buffon came he would
see her. I asked him "what he meant to do ?"
He said that he was very undecided, but that he
should like to know what really was going on
in Paris, and what they were doing, although
by this time his own people had confirmed
what my servant had said. He wished Prince
Louis D'Aremberg could see the Duc de
Biron ; that he then would hear something
more, which would decide his conduct for that
night.

Carriages were not allowed to pass through
the streets of Paris after ten o'clock. As the
Duke wished to be alone, I went with Prince
Louis to the Duc de Biron's on foot. We saw
many groups assembled in all the streets near
the Tuileries and Place Louis Quinze. I was
very anxious about the Duke's situation, and
wished much to know the public opinion about
him ; we therefore mixed in the groups, and of
course heard different sides of the question :
some were very violent in the Duke's favour,

others as violent against him, these latter accusing him of wanting to dethrone the King.

This accusation shocked me so much, that I returned directly to Monceau, and told him of what horrors they accused him. I found Madame de Buffon with him, and as her politics and mine were very different, I called the Duke into the garden, and we walked there till two o'clock. I entreated him on my knees to go directly to Versailles, and not to leave the King whilst Paris was in such a state of tumult; and by that conduct to show the King that the mob made use of his name without his knowledge or consent, and to express how shocked he was at what was going on, which I really thought he was. He said that "he could not go at so late an hour; that he had heard that the avenues were guarded, and that the King would be in bed, and could not be seen at that hour," but he gave me his word of honour that he would go at seven o'clock in the morning.

We did not find the Duc de Biron, nor did the Duke of Orleans see him that night. He had gone to Versailles in the evening, thinking to find the Duke there, or to hear of him, as he had a house in the Avenues, besides his apartments in the Palace, as first Prince of the Blood. I then went home, my house being near his; and I heard in the morning that the Duke had gone to Versailles.

On the Monday the Comte D'Artois, the Prince of Condé, and the Duke of Bourbon made their escape. They did perfectly right, for they certainly would have been murdered; but they did not at that moment mean or expect, perhaps, to leave their country for ever.

All that day, which was the 13th July, Paris was a scene of riot and horror. The murder of Messrs. De Foulon and Flesselles, Prevôts des Marchands, is too well known for me to relate. I was unfortunate enough to try to go to my jeweller's that evening, and I met in the Rue St. Honoré the soldiers of the French Guards carrying Monsieur de Foulon's head by the light of flambeaux. They thrust the head into my carriage: at the horrid sight I screamed and fainted away, and had I not had an English lady with me, who had courage enough to harangue the mob, and to say that I was an English patriot, they certainly would have murdered me; for they began to accuse me of being one of poor Foulon's friends, and of wishing the people to live on hay, of which they had accused him. I did not attempt to go further, but returned home almost dead. I was put to bed and bled, and indeed was very ill.

I soon afterwards received a note from the Duke of Orleans, begging me to go to him directly at Monceau, but I sent to the Duke telling him my situation. He came to me immediately, and was much alarmed to see me so ill. I asked him how he had been received at Versailles? and why he had returned so soon, as the States were then at Versailles in the Jeu de Paume, and he had apartments in the Château? He told me that on his arrival, he went directly to the King's levée, who was just getting up. The King took no notice of him; but as it was the custom for the first Prince of the Blood to give the King his shirt when he was present, the *gentilhomme de la chambre* gave the shirt to the Duke of Orleans to put over the King's head. The Duke approached the King, who asked him " what he wanted ?" The Duke, in passing the shirt, said, "I come to take your Majesty's commands." The King answered him, with great harshness, "I want nothing of *you*—return from whence you came." The Duke was very much hurt and very angry; and, leaving the room, went to the States, which I think were then sitting in the Jeu de Paume; and he returned to Paris at night.

He was much more out of humour than I had ever seen him. He said, that "the King and Queen disliked him, and that they would endeavour to poison him; that if he wished ever so much to be of use to the King and Queen, they never would believe him to be sincere; and that he never would go near them again, for he thought himself very cruelly used, as he really meant to be of use to the King; and had he been well received when he went to the levée, things might have been better for all parties, but now he should make friends of his own."

From that very instant, indeed, I thought

the Duke became more violent in politics; and
although I never heard him speak with dis-
respect of the King, I certainly have heard him
very, very violent against the Qüeen. I am
very sorry: the Court should have considered
the Duke's power, and been more cautious how
it offended him, for I am certain that at that
moment, had they treated him with consideration, and shown him more confidence, they
might have withdrawn him from the horrible
creatures who surrounded him—Talleyrand,
Mirabeau, the Duc de Biron, the Viscount de
Noailles, the Comte de la Mark, and others of
less note. These were the first who dragged
the Duke of Orleans into all the horrors of the
Revolution, though many of them forsook him
when they saw that he was unfit for their
projects. They left him, however, in worse
hands than their own; surrounded him with
monsters such as Laclos, Merlin de Douay,
and others, who never left him till they had
plunged him in dishonour, and led him to the
scaffold.

The Viscount de Noailles told me himself,

that it was he who introduced that monster Laclos to the Duke, and that he had recommended him as his secretary. This man was the cause of all the crimes which the Orleanist faction has been supposed to commit; and I am certain that the Duke knew little of what was going on in his name.

The Duke was a man of pleasure, who never could bear trouble or business of any kind; who never read or did anything but amuse himself. At that moment he was very madly in love with Madame de Buffon, driving her about all day in a curricle, and at all the *spectacles* in the evening; therefore he could not possibly be planning conspiracies. Indeed, the Duke's misfortune was to have been surrounded by ambitious men, who led him to their purpose by degrees, representing everything to him in a favourable light, and hurrying him on till he was so much in their power that he could not recede. Then they threatened to leave him, if he did not consent to their measures.

I am certain that the Duke never at that time had an idea of mounting the throne, what-

ever the views of his factious friends might
have been. If they could have placed him on
the throne of France, I suppose they hoped to
govern him and the country ; and they were
capable of any horrors to serve their own
purposes. The Duc de Biron excepted (and
he was too much led by Talleyrand), there
never was such a set of monsters as the unfortunate Duke's self-styled friends, who pretended
to be acting for the good of their country,
at the moment they were plotting its total
ruin.

Such were the people in whose hands the
Court had left the Duke. I say *left* ; for I am
persuaded that they might, at the beginning,
have got him out of the hands of those *in-
triguants*, by showing him attention and confidence. He was too powerful to be neglected.
Would that they had thought so too ! for it
would have saved the blood of the unfortunate
Royal Family, and, indeed, perhaps have saved
Europe from the dreadful scenes it has experienced since this horrid French Revolution.

The Duke of Orleans was a very amiable

and very high-bred man, with the best temper
in the world, but the most unfit man that ever
existed to be set up as a chief of a great faction. Neither his mind, his abilities, nor indeed
his education, fitted him for such an elevation;
and I long hoped that his heart revolted at the
idea of bringing his country into a state of
such cruel anarchy. His factious friends found
this out at last, for they never could get him to
attend to any of their projects; and some of
them were fortunate enough to make a sort of
peace with the Court; leaving the unhappy
Duke in the hands of those miscreants whom
they had placed about him, who brought others
with them like themselves, until they succeeded
in his total ruin and dishonour.

This I am grieved to say; for I had known
the Duke of Orleans for years, and he had
always been good and kind to me—as indeed he
was to everybody who approached him. I had
a sincere friendship for him, and would have
given my life to save him from dishonour.
Nobody can form an idea of what I suffered on
seeing him by degrees running headlong into

every sort of disgrace; for I am convinced,
from the bottom of my soul, that he never
thought or intended to go the lengths he
did.

I have the great comfort of knowing, that
from the first day of the horrors in Paris, I
always warned the Duke, and told him how it
would all end; and I have most awfully to
lament the little influence I possessed over him;
for I ever detested the Revolution, and those
who caused it. My conduct at that time is well
known to all the King and Queen's friends,
and by the French Princes now in England,
who will do me justice, though they know the
attachment I had for the Duke of Orleans, their
very gentle but unfortunate cousin. Even when
I saw him given up and shunned by everybody,
I received him, and tried to make him sensible
of his errors. He appeared sometimes as if he
felt that he was wrong, and I flattered myself
that he would leave it all; but he went from me
to Madame de Buffon, of whom he was very
fond, but whose politics, I am sorry to say, were
those of Laclos and Merlin, whom he always

found at her house, where he dined with them every day. They persuaded the pliant Duke that all which was going on was for the good of his country; and of course what I had said was forgotten. To my deep regret, I found he was so surrounded that he could not escape their snares, and that I did no good. He only laughed at me, saying that "I was a proud Scotchwoman, who loved nothing but kings and princes."

These thoughts have led me to digress: we will now return to the events which followed the 13th July, 1789. On the morning of the 14th, finding myself able to get up, I went by my garden to the Duke of Orleans, at Monceau, to try to see him before he went to the States. At his gate I found a hackney-coach in the first court, which surprised me, as hackney-coaches were not admitted there. I went directly into the garden, which was open. I saw the Duke in the room conversing with two men. On seeing me he came out, and asked me to make breakfast for him and the Marquis de Lafayette and Monsieur Bailly, two of his friends. I had known Lafayette at Strasbourg and in Paris, but had never seen the other man.

I found by their general conversation that they came to consult the Duke about the events which were going on in Paris, and I heard afterwards that on this same day Lafayette was made commander-in-chief, and Bailly mayor of Paris. Whilst we were at breakfast, we heard the cannon, and the report of the taking of the Bastille, on which these gentlemen went off in a great hurry. The Viscount de Noailles and the Duke de Biron came in directly afterwards, and as I saw I could have no conversation with the Duke, I went away. The Duke came into the garden with me. I had only time to entreat him to go once more to the King and offer his services. He was very angry with me, and asked me whether "I was paid by his enemies to give him such advice?" and left me directly.

I went home extremely unhappy, for I then saw that he was at open war with the King, which was what I dreaded the most, as from that moment I considered him entirely in the hands of his factious followers. In the course of that day the Bastille was taken, Monsieur de Launay and others were murdered, every sort of brutal excess was committed, and scenes of horror were occurring every hour. The mob obliged everybody to wear a green cockade for two days, but afterwards they took red, white, and blue, the Orleans livery. The streets, all the evening of the 14th, were in an uproar; the French Guards and all those who were at the taking of the Bastille, were mad drunk, dragging dead bodies and heads and limbs about the streets by torch-light. The same day they went to the country-house of M. Berthier, the Intendant of Paris, and forced him into a cabriolet to take him to Paris. When they got near Paris, a fresh mob, with some of the French Guards, met him, and with sabres cut off the top of the cabriolet. They then beat him and pelted him, and cut his legs and face. When they got him to the Porte St. Martin, they brought his father-in-law's (M. Foulon's) head, and made him kiss it, and then they forced him to get out

D

of the cabriolet, and hung him up to a lantern. They then dragged his body through the streets, and carried his head to the house of his father-in-law, where Madame Berthier, his poor wife, was lying-in. They took the head into her room; and she expired that same evening from the fright.

Such were the dreadful scenes of that day!

CHAPTER II.

Conversations with the Duke of Orleans—Sketch of Marie-
Antoinette—Unpopularity of the Duke of Orleans with the
Court—He visits England—The Netherland Revolutionists
— My Passport stopped — Colonel Gardiner, English
Minister at Brussels—Gross insult offered to the British
Government—Interview with the Belgian Revolutionary
Leaders — Infamous Conduct of Capuchin Priests—My
Return to Paris—The Festival of the Federation at the
Champ-de-Mars—Louis XVI.—Marie-Antoinette—Talley-
rand—The Duke of Orleans daily drifting into the hands
of the most violent Revolutionists—Conversations with
the Duke—Marie-Antoinette visits my House and Gardens — Intrusted with a Commission by Marie-Antoinette—The *Chevaliers de la Poignard*—A Leader wanted
for the Royalists.

FROM this period I saw little of the Duke of
Orleans. I went to the château of a friend of
mine at Ivry, near Paris. Many events happened
in the course of the summer, known to all
those who have read the history of the French
Revolution. My object being only to give
some anecdotes of the Duke of Orleans, I will

not pretend to detail all the events which took place; nor indeed could any pen give an adequate description of them, or any idea of that horrid and bloody period, which is a disgrace to human nature.

The Duke came twice to dine with me in the country, and I found his manner much altered. He was low-spirited, which never was his natural character. I always expressed great uneasiness to him on account of his situation; at which he laughed, and said that " I was very foolish, and that he had no reason to be uneasy; that I was like all the aristocrats, and wanted to thwart popular opinion; that he never was angry with people on account of their opinions about the Revolution, and wished that people would leave him alone."

In October I left Ivry, and stayed in Paris all the winter. My house being near Monceau, I saw the duke very often; but as I perceived that what I said displeased him, I thought it best not to talk politics, when I could avoid it. At that moment I flattered myself that those horrible revolutionary principles would soon have an end, either by the French people finding out their own miserable situation, and rallying round their monarch, or by the assistance of foreign troops. Though I dreaded the storm which then would have fallen on the Duke, yet I must own, and indeed I have often told him so, that I should prefer to hear of his perpetual imprisonment, even of his death, rather than to see him degraded and dishonoured.

Soon after this came the 5th of October, a memorable and dreadful day. But I must here do justice to the Duke of Orleans. He certainly was not at Versailles on that dreadful morning, for he breakfasted with company at my house, when he was accused of being in the Queen's apartments disguised. He told us then that he heard the fishwomen had gone to Versailles with some of the Fauxbourgs, and that people said they were gone to bring the King again to Paris. He informed us that he had heard this from some of his own servants from the Palais Royal. He said he was the more surprised at this, as he had left the Palais Royal gardens at nine o'clock of the night before, and all then seemed perfectly quiet. He expressed himself as not approving of their bringing the King to Paris; "that it must be a scheme of Lafayette's;" but added, " I dare say that they will accuse me of it, as they lay every tumult to my account. I think myself this is a mad project, and like all that Lafayette does." He stayed at my house till half-past one o'clock. I have no reason to suppose that he went to Versailles till late in the day, when he went to the States, as everybody knows. The unfortunate King and Queen were brought to Paris that evening by Lafayette's mob.

I have entered into this subject that I may have an opportunity of declaring that I firmly believe the Duke of Orleans was innocent of the cruel events of that day and night; and that Lafayette was the author and instigator of the treatment the august Royal Family then met with. If the Duke of Orleans' greatest enemies will be candid, I am sure that they must acquit him of the events of that day,—a day, which, in my opinion, decided the fate of the Royal Family, and which showed the country what dreadful events might be expected from such a set of monsters. The Duke of Orleans was even tried on this account, but the proofs were so absurd that it was dropped. And indeed it was clear to everybody, that Lafayette and his party were the only guilty people.

It is well known that the King and Queen were never again allowed to return to Versailles. They were not even permitted to go to St. Cloud, though their health and that of their children required country air. They used to allow the poor Queen, as a great favour, to go out in her coach and six, accompanied by the Dauphin and Madame Royale, Madame Elizabeth, and Madame de Tourzelle. On these occasions they always looked dismal and unhappy; indeed they had every reason to be so, for very few showed the Queen the least respect. Even those who some months before would have lain down in the dust to make a footstool for her, passed her and splashed her all over. I used frequently to meet her Majesty when I was driving my curricle. Of

course I showed her every mark of respect in
my power, at which she expressed herself much
pleased.   Indeed she had the condescension to
send one of her equerries, M. de Chatiers, after
me, to ask me how my daughter was, as her
Majesty had been good enough to think her a
beautiful child, and to take great notice of her
when she was about three years old, at St. Cloud,
and had sent the Duke de Liancourt for her,
and kept her upon her knee all the time their
Majesties were at dinner.   From that moment
I always felt myself obliged to the Queen for
her kindness to my child.

I believe that she was as amiable and good
a princess as ever lived. She was cruelly
slandered by the French nation.   I have
known intimately those who attended nearest
to her Majesty's person, and from whom she
hid nothing, and they assured me that she
was goodness itself—a kind and most affectionate mistress.   Indeed she was too much so
to many who did not deserve her kindness.
The Queen's misfortune was that she had been
brought very young to the Court of Louis the

Fifteenth, where she was exposed to scenes of levity and improper society. She had thus imbibed a taste for fashions and public amusements, which she could not have enjoyed, had she kept up her etiquette as a great queen. By this means she made herself many enemies amongst the formal old ladies of the Court, whom she disliked, and attached herself to younger people, whose taste was more suited to her own. This was never forgiven by the old nobility, and her most innocent actions were represented in a bad light; her enemies, indeed, accused her of every sort of vice. But let them reflect one moment on those who formed the Queen's most intimate society. It was Madame Elizabeth, the King's sister, who was an angel, and as pure as snow. Was she likely to have connived in the Queen's dishonour? The idea is horrid; yet the parties at Trianon, which were made so much the subject of calumny, were always under the management of that virtuous princess. Madame Elizabeth's attachment for the Queen continued till her last moments, which I think proves more

than sufficient for the unfortunate Queen's vindication. Lafayette's treatment of the Royal
Family during their captivity in the Tuileries
was very harsh. He was always raising reports of their wishing to escape, that he might
make himself of consequence both to the royalists and his friends the *rebels*. These reports
always ended in some new insult shown to the
Royal Family.

At this time the Duke of Orleans became
more and more execrated by the Court and the
royalists, without having more power in his own
party, who were constantly making use of his
name while committing horrors in conjunction
with Lafayette's party; and I must here again
declare I do not believe that what was called
the Orleans faction ever even consulted the unfortunate Duke about their proceedings. Soon
after this the Court seemed to treat the Duke
a little better, and the King appointed him
High Admiral of France, which surprised
people at that moment. However, his favour
did not last. The King about that time was
very ill with a cold, and kept his bed at the

Tuileries. Of course all the nobility went to pay their respects to his Majesty. The Duke of Orleans went also. When the King heard that he was there, he said, "Let the Duke of Orleans approach my bed, and let all the curtains be opened, that he may see that it is I; or a report will be raised in Paris that I have fled, and that somebody else was in the bed." This anecdote the Duke told me himself, and he was much displeased with the King on that account.

Soon after this the ministers and the Court thought that if they could get the Duke out of Paris things would be quieter. They supposed him to have more partisans than he really had, and also more power. It was at this time that they conceived the idea of the Duke being made Duke of Brabant—a very ridiculous plan. I believe, however, that the Duke was foolish enough to consent to it, and, indeed, to wish it much. For that purpose they gave him a sort of mission to England, but on what subject I never positively knew, as I never conversed with the Duke on that matter. Our ministers must know what brought him to England. Many ill-natured reports were spread in Paris, such as asserting that Lafayette had forced the Duke to leave Paris, as he had proofs that the Duke had attempted to get the King assassinated. This was false, as the Duke and Lafayette were at that moment good friends, and had met as friends the evening before the Duke went to England at Madame de Coigny's, where they were on the best of terms. I have some letters of Lafayette to the Duke since that period, full of respect and compliments.

In the spring of 1790 I went to Brussels, and saw many of the Duke's agents, such as Comte de la Mark, Walgains the banker, and others; but I soon found out that the Comte was more active with a view of becoming Duke of Brabant himself, or at least of getting the dukedom into his own family. I saw him as active in that revolution as he has been in France. That country was then in full revolt against the Emperor. There were two rebel parties, the Vandernotts and the Vonckists: the first were so on religious pretexts, and the others were more inclined to the Jacobins of France. This party was the one which was supposed to favour the Duke of Orleans ; and of this party were the D'Arembergs. I had an opportunity of seeing both Vandernott and Vannpar [qy.], who was a monk of the order of the Penitents, and always wore the habit. He was a very clever, artful man, and under the mask of religion led the others. Vandernott was an *avocat*, very quick and active, and was the chief actor under Vannpar.

At that period people who resided at Brussels were obliged to have a pass to go out of town. On sending one day to the town-house to get one to go to the Duke d'Aremberg at Enghien, between Halle and Condé, they sent me word that they had orders not to let me go out of the town. I was much surprised and shocked at this, as I considered myself an English subject. I went immediately to Colonel Gardiner, our Minister at Brussels, to complain. He said that " he was not surprised at anything the States did ; that they had some days before stopped his own messenger going to

England, and had broken open his despatches; that he had been to the States to complain, but had had no redress; that he did not mean to go to them any more till he heard from his Court what he was to do; and that if I insisted on his going on my account he would, but he thought he had better not." I said, I had a great mind to go myself to Vandernott, as I used often to meet him, and he always bowed to me.   Colonel Gardiner thought that I should do right.   I went accordingly that same day, and found Vandernott and Vannpar together.   I sent in my name, and was very well received.   I stated my complaint, and that as as a subject of the King of England they had used me ill. He said that " he had never given such orders; that other members must have done it; that he was so much harassed by business that he could not be answerable for every fault that was committed.   He was very sorry, and assured me I should from that moment have a pass to go and come from Enghien whenever I pleased."   At the same time he told me that " he knew I was come from

Paris, and there saw much of the Duke of
Orleans, and at Brussels lived a great deal
with the D'Arembergs, and of course was of
their party." I assured him that " I was not ;
that though I saw much of those people, yet I
never had liked their revolutionary conduct
either in France or Brabant ; that I always
was a royalist, and ever should be such ; that I
was neither a Vandernottist nor a Vonckist.
Both Vandernott and Vannpar smiled, and said
" at least I was very honest ; but as there were
very few royalists in Brussels I was not dangerous, and they would not disturb me any
more." They were in high good humour, as
that very day they had received news of a
victory over Vandermerck, a Vonckist general.

The villagers were beginning to enter Brussels in procession, bringing large baskets filled
with gold of all coins, to give to Vandernott
to carry on the revolution. These processions
were followed by monks of all orders, Capuchins,
&c., on horseback with a cross in one hand and
a sword in the other. They were closed by the
hangmen of the villages and towns, carrying

gallows and racks. In the evening these poor deluded people returned to their villages drunk and in complete riot.

I witnessed many terrible scenes in Brussels, similar to those in France, but here religion was the pretext. I saw poor creatures murdered in the streets because they did not pull their hats off to Capuchins, or for passing a bust of Vandernott without bowing very low. His busts were put all over the town and even in the theatre. Vandernott was a very odd-looking man. He was, I fancy, about forty, rather tall and thin. He was full of vivacity, and did not look ill-natured, though very ugly. I never shall forget his dress. It was a Quaker-coloured silk coat lined with pink and narrow silver-lace, a white dimity waistcoat, white cotton stockings, net ruffles with fringe round them, and a powdered bob-wig.

The horrors now began to gain ground in Brussels. The Austrians got possession of the town, but were unfortunately driven out again by the patriots. There was a truce one night. During this time the poor Austrians were lying in the Park of Brussels, without food or anything they wanted, for the inhabitants of Brussels did not dare even to sell them an ounce of bread. Here they lay all night in the wet. As my house was in the Park, I gave them out of the window everything that was in the house of eatables and drink; and so did Prince Louis d'Aremberg, though it was not his brother's party, he having always remained a staunch royalist.

As I feared when the Austrians left Brussels that I might be ill-used by the mob, I set off for Paris the next day, hoping to remain there quiet. At this time the Duke of Orleans was in England, but his enemies having propagated stories of his not daring to return to France, his friend the Duc de Biron pressed him much to return, and show the world that he was not afraid of Lafayette. I was in Paris when the Duke returned, which was the 13th of July, 1790, at night. The following day, the 14th, was the first famous Federation, when the King and Queen went to the Champ de Mars, and when Monsieur de Talleyrand,

E

then Bishop of Autun, said mass before their
Majesties. The Duke of Orleans walked in the
procession, and people were much surprised to
see him, after the reports which had been circulated.

I saw him that same day. He dined with me,
as did the Duc de Biron and others. He had
brought me letters from England, where he
had seen my daughter. The Duke expressed
much regret at leaving England: would to
to God that he had stayed there! He was,
however, rather well received at Paris; but his
faction was always afraid lest he should be better
treated by the Court, and so slip through their
fingers. They were enchanted at his having
been very much insulted one day at Court, as
they saw that they had nothing more to fear
from that quarter; and the Duke by that means
became every day more and more in their power.

I wish that the Court would have believed
me. The Queen had very often expressed her
approbation, and indeed had sent me kind mes-
sages as to my conduct during the Revolution.
She well knew the advice I always gave the Duke

of Orleans; indeed her Majesty charged me once with a *mission* to Brussels, which showed the opinion she honoured me with, though she knew that I saw the Duke every day. I always hoped to be of use, but alas! I did not succeed. Madame de Buffon and the Duke's friends did everything they could to prevent his coming to me. They used to tell him that as I saw none but royalists and his enemies, I should get him assassinated. However, he never would give me up; and though he heard nothing but harsh truth from me, he always came to me, and he always assured me that he believed I was sincere in thinking I gave him good advice, but that the royalists had turned my head, and would cause my ruin. I wish that he had believed in my foresight, for I often foretold him what has since happened.

I took at that time a house at Issy, near Paris, which belonged to the Duchess St. Infantador. She, poor woman, had been a friend of the Queen, who used often to go to Issy with her children to walk in the grounds. It was a beautiful place, and there her Majesty could

enjoy a little quiet, without being followed by a
crowd of National Guards. The people of the
village accused the Duchess of hiding effects of
the Court and royalists, and used to go in the
dead of the night and search the house.   This
.plagued her so much, that she left France and
returned to Spain, leaving orders that her
house might be let. I took it for two years,
but the village was so Jacobin that I left it,
and bought a small cottage at Meudon, some
miles further. The Queen came twice to Issy
while I had it, and was always condescending
enough to ask my leave to walk in the
grounds.

Her Majesty, hearing that I had thoughts of
returning to Brussels, sent a great lady to my
house with a small box and a letter for the
Archduchess, which I was to deliver into her
own hands. I did not intend going to Brussels,
but I never made that known to her Majesty.
I got a passport from Lord Gower, our ambassador, and felt myself happy in taking this
journey to be of use to the Queen. When I
got to Brussels, the Archduchess had just left it

with the Duke Albert; and as the Queen had
foreseen the possibility of this, she had desired
me in that case to deliver it to General Boileau,
who was at Mons, commanding the Austrian
army.

The Queen's coming to Issy gave rise to a
report that her Majesty had had a conversation
with the Duke at Issy. The Duke would often
dine with me there, and indeed often met the
young nobles who had returned to Paris from
Germany or England, in hopes of being of use
to the King. But all their plans were ill-con-
ceived and very ill-executed, turning out always
to the unfortunate King's disadvantage, as they
gave the conspirators an opportunity of con-
fining the King and his family more severely.
I was always uneasy when the Duke came and
the royalists were present, as I was afraid of the
Duke meeting with any insult in my house.
That would have made me miserable. But as
politics were never discussed, and the Duke was
very civil and good-natured to them, nothing
disagreeable happened; though the young men,
as well as the Duke, seemed much embarrassed.

They had all been his intimate friends before the Revolution, and had liked and respected him much ; therefore their situation was more distressing. These nobles were what were called *Les Chevaliers de la Poignard.*

Everybody must remember the day when they rallied round the King at the Tuileries, a project which was not of the least use. They wanted numbers, and an able chief. Had any prince of the Bourbons come to Paris, or planted a standard to make a rallying point for the royalists in any part of France, I really think the King might have been delivered ; but very unfortunately there was no one chief on whom they could depend.

I myself, since the reign of Bonaparte, have heard General Leopold Berthier, brother to the Minister at War, say that he and his brother would have repaired to any standard where there was a chief of the House of Bourbon, and have fought for the King to the last drop of their blood. I have heard other generals say as much. I am certain that three parts, at least, of France would have done the same.

What a misfortune for the world that this was not the case! Even the brave and loyal Vendéans were sacrificed for want of a proper chief. That valiant and hardy people, in spite of all the calamities they had suffered, would ever have been ready to rise for the royal cause. Their loyalty and religion will always keep them faithful subjects.

The King, poor man, had now little exercise. When he rode out, accompanied by the few friends he had left, such as the Duc de Brisac, the Chevalier de Coigny, and others, that wretch Lafayette always followed him with twenty or thirty of the officers of the National Guards, so that he seldom went out, as his rides were not comfortable in such company.

CHAPTER III.

Conduct of Monsieur, since Louis XVIII.—Gentleness of
Louis XVI.—Royal Family escape to Varennes—Brought
back to Paris—Their brutal treatment by the Mob—
Position of the Duke of Orleans—His disposition—He joins
the Army—The Mob break into the Tuileries, and insult
the King—Marie-Antoinette's last appearance in public—
The 10th of August—My Flight to Meudon—Return to
Paris—Adventures—Murder of the Swiss Guards—Extraordinary escape of Marquis de Chansenets.

MONSIEUR, now Louis XVIII. was in Paris
during all these events; but he lived a great
deal with people of letters, and seldom left the
Luxembourg but to go to the Tuileries. Many
have blamed this prince for his conduct when
he went to the Hotel de Ville; but I am certain,
and everybody is now convinced of it, that his
motive for so doing was the hope of being of
use to the unfortunate King, his brother.
These were most certainly virtuous motives,
although not attended with success. This

prince has always been much respected by the King's friends, and those who blamed him the most saw that the motive was good.

The friends of Lafayette were ever talking of the King's escape. Would to God that he had succeeded in getting off! It would have spared France from many crimes, and saved the life of that virtuous monarch, who was too good to reign over such miscreants. He was religious, and could not bear to shed the blood of his subjects; for had he, when the nobles went over to the Tiers États, caused the unfortunate Duke of Orleans, and about twenty others, to be arrested and executed, Europe would have been saved from the calamities it has since suffered; and I should now dare to regret my poor friend the Duke, who, instead of dying thus regretted, lived to be despised and execrated, and to perish on a scaffold by the hands of those whom he had dishonoured himself to serve. These are cruel truths for me to tell, but such they are.

Everybody knows that in the summer of 1791 the King and royal family tried to make their escape. I have no doubt that Lafayette was privy to the event, and afterwards through fear betrayed him. They were stopped at Varennes, used most cruelly, and brought back to Paris in a most barbarous manner. I saw them in the Champs Elysées as they came back, and witnessed such a scene as it is impossible to describe. The insolence of the mob and the wretches that surrounded the travelling coaches they were in was very terrible. The faithful Garde de Corps, who had followed the King, were tied hands and feet with ropes on the coach-box of their Majesties' carriage, which went at a foot-pace, that the monsters might follow. They were leaning on the coach, smoking, swearing, and talking the most indecent language. They prevented any air getting into the carriage, though the poor Queen was dying with heat and fatigue, for they had not been in bed since they left Paris, and it was one of the hottest days I ever felt. This was another dreadful event.

I left Paris that evening for Spa, and found Monsieur, now Louis XVIII., at Brussels.

He had succeeded in making his escape by Valenciennes. I wish that the King had taken that road and gone alone, but he never could be persuaded to leave the Queen, as he feared that the mob would murder her. I stayed at Spa till September. Would that I had never again returned to France! But at that moment we expected the Prussians, the Austrians, and Swedes to join and save France from any further faction; for though the King's arrest at Varennes had much damped the spirits of the royalists, the case was too interesting to be given up. Spa was full of emigrants, and they all expected soon to return to France. The unfortunate King of Sweden, who was himself assassinated some months after, was a sincere friend to the King of France, and would have aided the counter-revolution with all his power. I knew him, and thought him one of the best-bred and most amiable men I ever saw.

On my return to Paris I found that many of the emigrants had entered France in hopes of a change, but Lafayette and his friends had so surrounded both the outside and inside of the

King's palace with spies, that it was hardly possible for the friends of the King or Queen to have any communication with them ; and their projects were again and again frustrated.

I cannot recollect any other events of that year, except that on my return to Paris I found the Duc de Choiseul and the Comte Charles de Damas had been arrested for being colonels of the two regiments which were to have favoured the King's escape. I had a letter given me at Spa by Comte Roger Damas for his brother, and I was determined to deliver it into his own hands, for fear it might contain anything about the passing events. He was imprisoned at the Mercy, a convent of Brothers in the Marais. I obtained admission there, and saw both him and the Duc de Choiseul. They were in very low spirits, but the King got them relieved soon after.

After this, I remained always either at Issy or in Paris, till I bought my house at Meudon. I often saw the Duke of Orleans, but was so disappointed at the very unfortunate turn everything took for the royal cause, that I avoided as much as possible listening to anything on the subject. I observed also how the Duke was daily lowering himself. I was, indeed, very unhappy. His faction, and of course himself, were accused of the disturbances which were going on. That faction, without the Duke, was capable of anything; still I do not believe that all the riots were committed by it. Lafayette did much harm.

The Duke of Orleans was taxed with having given large sums of money at the beginning of the Revolution to incite the French Guards to revolt. This I do not believe; nor could those who examined his papers and affairs after his death ever find any evidence of this having been the case. Those who made this examination were not the Duke's friends, and would not have spared him could they have found it out. There were in his accounts only thirteen thousand livres for which they could not account; but so small a sum could not have paid such a body of men. Lafayette himself incited them to revolt. I am certain, that had the Duke of Orleans expected the Revolution to last more than six months, he never would have wished it. He had the great fault of not forgiving easily. His governor, the Comte de Pons, when he had finished the Duke's education, and he went out of his hands, made use of this expression : " I have finished the education of a young prince who will make a noise, but he must not be offended—he does not pardon." This, however, was not quite the case, for I have seen him forgive ; and never saw him nor heard him say any ill-natured thing to anybody until his head was turned by the horrid Revolution.

In the year 1792, the Duke went to join the French Army du Nord, commanded by the old Comte de Rochambeau. He had his three sons with him ; at least, Monsieur le Duc de Mont pensier and the Comte de Beaujolais. I think that the Duc de Chartres was then more advanced in Brabant with Dumourier, but I cannot remember the events of the army. The poor Royal Family got worse used every day : their existence indeed was terrible. When the French army was defeated at Mons, the Duc de Biron commanded, and the Dukes of Chartres and Montpensier were with him. It was their first campaign, and I remember that it was after this period the Duke of Orleans went to join the army at Courtray, and took his youngest son, Comte de Beaujolais, with him.

In the course of this summer, the 20th of June, the Poissardes and the Fauxbourgs, headed by Santerre, came down to the Tuileries, and forced their way into the King's apartments, as the King would never allow the troops to fire on the mob; indeed, most part of the troops were National Guards, who were no better than the mob that came. These miscreants forced the red cap on the King's head, and used gross and familiar language to him. They wanted to get to the Queen's apartments, as was supposed to murder her. It was Madame Elizabeth who prevented them. However, the Queen was frightened, and came and placed herself by the King's side, to whom she always fled for protection. They brought a little red cap for the dear little Dauphin. He was present, dressed in the regimentals of the nation, for they had formed a corps of little boys which was called the Prince Dauphin's regiment. In short, this mob, after staying a great part of the evening, annoying the King and Queen, drinking and stealing everything they could lay their hands on, quitted the Palace, and left the Royal Family convinced that they had now nothing to expect but similar insults.

At that period I received a letter from the Duke of Orleans, who was then at Courtray, which letter I have now before me, expressing his satisfaction at being out of Paris at that moment. In it he says: "I hope they will not now accuse me;" but if he was innocent, his friends perhaps were not; and the gross insult offered to the King at the Palace was imputed to Robespierre and Marat, who never were even of the Orleans faction. After the 20th of June, the people who wished well to the King and Queen were desirous that her Majesty should sometimes appear in public, accompanied by the Dauphin, a most interesting, beautiful child, and her charming daughter,

Madame Royale. In consequence of this she
went to the Comédie Italienne with her
children, Madame Elizabeth, the King's sister
and Madame Tourzelle, governess to the royal
children. This was the very last time on which
her Majesty appeared in public. I was there
in my own box, nearly opposite the Queen's;
and as she was so much more interesting than
the play, I never took my eyes off her and
her family. The opera which was given was
Les Evénemens Imprévus, and Madame Dugazon
played the *soubrette*. Her Majesty, from her
first entering the house, seemed distressed. She
was overcome even by the applause, and I saw
her several times wipe the tears from her eyes.
The little Dauphin, who sat on her knee the
whole night, seemed anxious to know the cause
of his unfortunate mother's tears. She seemed
to soothe him, and the audience appeared well
disposed, and to feel for the cruel situation of
their beautiful Queen. In one of the acts a
duet is sung by the *soubrette* and the *valet*,
where Madame Dugazon says: '*Ah! comme
j'aime ma maîtresse!*' As she looked particularly

F

at the Queen at the moment she said this, some
Jacobins, who had come into the playhouse,
leapt upon the stage, and if the actors had not
hid Madame Dugazon, they would have murdered her. They hurried the poor Queen and
family out of the house, and it was all the
Guards could do to get them safe into their
carriages. By this time the Queen's party
began to beat the Jacobins, but the soldiers
interfered, and of course nothing could be done.
This was, I say, her Majesty's last appearance
in public. There were very few indeed at the
theatre that night who had not made a point
of going on purpose to applaud the Royal
Family; but the Jacobins finding that, sent for
their own people to insult this interesting
family.

The next event which occurred was the 10th
of August, never to be forgotten! As I was
getting up I heard a great cannonading. My
house being in the Faubourg St. Honoré, not
far from the Tuileries, the noise was terrible. I
soon heard the dreadful news that the Faubourgs
St. Antoine and St. Marceau, having Santerre

at their head, had marched down and attacked the Tuileries ; that the King and Queen had fled to the National Assembly ; in short, I heard of the horrors which were going on. My first wish was to leave Paris, and go to my house at Meudon, but I was told that the barriers of Paris were shut, and no one was allowed to go out of the town.

In the course of the morning I had an opportunity of being of use to three or four Swiss soldiers, whom I hid in my house till the evening : Major Backman living in the Rue Verte, and his garden and mine joining, they had come over the wall. I wish I could have done as much for their major, but he, poor man, perished that same day. I don't know whether the men who were hidden in my house were saved. They would go away in the evening, and I never heard of them more. My maid put me in mind of a porter of mine, who had taken a garden and small house behind the Invalides, and near the Military School. She said that she had often heard him declare that there was a breach in the walls of Paris close to

him, which the smugglers had made, and that
any one with little trouble could get over. I
desired my maid to say nothing to my servants
about this, but at nine o'clock to walk with me
to this man's house, who was a very honest and
good creature.   When I got there he seemed
afraid of assisting me, for fear of a discovery ; but
I promised him secresy, and that my maid should
return to my house in Paris, and that I would
go alone. I could not take her with me, as
everything I had was in Paris, and my house
at Meudon being small I kept few servants
there.

I got safely over the wall, crossed the plains
of Vaugirard in the dark, in fear every moment
of meeting patrole or murderers, till I got to
the bottom of the steep hill which leads up to
the Château of Meudon, my house being on the
top of the hill. I had never looked back : my
heart beat hard. I thought every moment
that I was followed. About the middle of the
hill I saw a man coming towards me, and was
so much terrified that I dropped down amongst
the vines which border the hill, quite losing

my senses. On my recovery I neither saw nor heard anybody. Perhaps it was some poor wretch making his escape, who was as much alarmed as I was. I was then not very far from my own house, and with great pain I reached it, but so much fatigued and agitated that they were obliged to undress me and put me to bed almost senseless.   My feet were covered with blood, having no soles to my shoes or stockings. My shoes were thin white silk, and that road is very stony.

I remained at Meudon as quiet and retired as I could till the dreadful 2nd of September. In the morning of that day a boy, who looked like a beggar, brought me a note from a friend of mine, entreating me to come to Paris, and to bring a passport with me for myself and servant, and to come alone, as I might by that means be of use to an unhappy person ; stating that if I wished to be of service I must come directly.   I did not hesitate, but went at once to the mayor of Meudon, who gave me a passport for myself and servant, to return before twelve o'clock at night. I got into one of the cabriolets which hold two people with a driver on the outside, and I went quite alone.   When I reached the Barrier Vaugirard, which is in the section of the Croix Rouge, and was one of the worst in Paris, I showed the guards my pass by which I was to return at night.   They said that I must go to the section-house, and get it signed.   The soldiers seemed surprised at my wishing to enter Paris at such a moment. They told me that the people were murdering in the prisons; that the streets were running in blood; and that those who were in Paris would give all they had in the world to be out of it. I told them that I had a mother dying, who wished to see me, and that I could not refuse to go to her.   They pitied me, and were very good-natured.

I then went to the section-house. I forgot to mention that they asked me for my servant at the barrier, and I told them that he had been sent back for some papers, which I was taking to my mother.   The guard, who went with me to the section-house, stated this, and of course they were not very suspicious about a person who wished to enter Paris at such a moment. I then went directly to my friend's house in the Rue de l'Encre, on the Boulevards de l'Ancienne Opéra, and I found to my very great surprise that the person she wished me to serve was the Marquis de Chansenets, governor of the Tuileries, who had been concealed in the roof of her house since the 10th of August.

I had heard, as had many others, that he had been murdered in the palace on the 10th. However, he had been fortunate enough to escape. He had passed the night between the 9th and 10th with the King in the interior of the palace, and of course was in his uniform, which was that of major-general. The troops in the palace were the brave and magnificent regiment of Swiss Guards, and the brave battalion of St. Thomas du Louvre, who all fought with great courage, till they found that the King and his family were gone, and that they had no more to do. The Swiss Guards and the battalion of St. Thomas were cut to pieces. Those who were left were

murdered by the mob, as were the officers.
Some indeed were beheaded. Monsieur de
Chansenets never left their Majesties till the
King was persuaded by Rœderer to fly to the
Assembly for protection for his family. The
Queen showed much reluctance to take such a
step, and did everything in her power to
prevent the King going, and even went on her
knees to him, but he thought that it would save
the blood of his subjects, and that his family
would be in safety, for I firmly believe that he
never considered himself in the matter. When
the unfortunate Queen left the palace, she gave
her hand to Monsieur de Chansenets, and said,
"I fear we are doing wrong, but you know that
I cannot persuade. Adieu! God only knows
if ever we shall meet again!"

After their departure, Chansenets had only
time to try to make his escape, as the troops
and the mob had got into the Palace, and were
murdering everybody belonging to the King,
and pillaging everything which came in their
way. Poor Chansenets, finding that he had no
chance of escape, being so well known as

governor of the Palace, threw himself out of one of the low windows into the garden, which was heaped with the bodies of the poor Swiss soldiers and others. There he lay amongst the dead and wounded all day, not daring to stir. At the time the weather was so very hot that the stench of the bodies became terrible in a few hours.

Towards evening one of the National Guards, who went to look amongst the dead and wounded for one of his friends, found that Monsieur Chansenets was alive. He knew him, and told him to get up, and he would lend him his coat, and remain himself in a waistcoat. He then recommended him to make his escape as well as he could, for that he could give him no further aid; and that what he was then doing would perhaps cost him his life. Chansenets went as fast as he could out of the garden by the Carrousel, almost fainting with fatigue, heat, want of food and rest. When he had reached the Rue de l'Échelle he could go no further. A poor woman who was standing at her shop-door asked him in, supposing him to be one of the soldiers tired. He told her that he was an Englishman; that curiosity had led him into the palace in the course of the day; that the mob had used him ill, and that a National soldier had lent him his coat. He assured her that he had been all day without food, and begged her to give him a crust of bread and a drop of brandy. As he spoke bad French, with an English accent, she believed him; but she told him that he must not stay there, as she expected her husband home every instant, and she said that he was a Jacobin, and detested gentlemen. She added, that she was sure by the fineness of his linen he was a noble; that her husband had been very busy all day murdering the Swiss soldiers and the King's friends; and that she would not at all wish him to fall into her husband's hands, as he hated also the English. The woman had not had time to get the bread when her husband came home. She had just time to put him behind a press. She, however, had the presence of mind to stop her husband at the door and tell him that one of his friends was anxious to see him, and was waiting for him at a cabaret just by.

The moment the man was gone she pushed Chansenets into the street without saying a word. It was then night, and he considered that if he could crawl to Lord Gower's, who was the English ambassador then in Paris, he might there meet with some means of hiding himself at least for the night. The ambassador lived in the Fauxbourg St. Germains on the new Boulevards.

On Chansenets' arrival there he saw Mr. Huskisson, Lord Gower's secretary, who was very kind to him, and went to inform Lord Gower of his being there. Lord Gower, however, as a public man, and not knowing what was to become of himself, could not receive him, as a strong proclamation had been published that night, and read by a man on horseback in the streets, prohibiting everybody, on pain of death, to receive or give any aid to the proscribed people who were with the King in the Tuileries, and thus pointing most at Monsieur de Chansenets as governor. Mr. Huskisson

lent him clothes.   When he left Lord Gower's
he hardly knew what to do ; nor had he any
idea where to go.   At last he recollected
having seen some time before an English lady
at my house, who lived very retired and kept
but one maid, and her lodging was in a part
of Paris very private. He thought that he might
venture to go to her, and try if she could by
any means hide him for that night, as he had
no creature else to whom he could apply; for
his other friends had many servants, who I am
sorry to say were little to be trusted.

My friend's lodging was in the Rue de l'Encre
behind the old Opera-house.   She lived up four
pair.   Chansenets got to her house late, having
gone through by-streets.   The porter at the
lodge, who always draws a string, there being
other lodgers in the house, only asked, " Who's
there?" Chansenets said, " Monsieur Smith, for
Madame Meyler," and as she was at home he
went up.   She was much surprised and terrified
at seeing him, having heard in the day that he
was killed.   He had never been in her house
before, but as he knew that she was a very good-

natured woman and a good royalist, he ran no
risk. She heard and saw his distress with
horror, for he was in a most deplorable state.
She had no means of hiding him, yet she could
not bear the idea of turning him into the
streets at that late hour, when he must have
been taken by the bloodhounds who were in
search for him. Her maid was a very faithful
old woman, and also a royalist; they therefore thought it best to confide in her, and tell
her what an unfortunate man she then had in
her power. She then assured him that as he
had had such confidence in her she certainly
thought she could hide him in the roof of the
room she lay in; but that she feared the people
who lived in the house might hear him; besides,
that the porter had seen him go in and had told
her that there was a gentleman upstairs with
her mistress. They therefore both went down
to the door with Chansenets as if he were
going away, and wished him good-night. Mrs.
Meyler stood at the door of the porter's lodge
and talked to him, whilst her old woman
pretended to let a little dog into the street,

during this time Chansenets slipped up-
stairs ; in short they hid him as well as they
could that night.

The same bloody scenes continued the next
day in Paris. Poor Laporte, the Intendant of
Finances, was executed, as well as many others,
officers of the Swiss Guards. The same pro-
clamations were read in the streets against the
Governor of the Tuileries, the Prince de Poix,
&c. The fate of the unfortunate Royal Family
was decided upon — they were sent to the
Temple. Domiciliary visits were made in most
parts of Paris.*   Mrs. Meyler not knowing

---

* Let the reader fancy to himself a vast metropolis, the
streets of which were a few days before alive with the con-
course of carriages, and with citizens constantly passing and
repassing, suddenly struck with the dead silence of the grave,
before sunset, on a fine summer evening. All the shops are
shut ; everybody retires into the interior of his house, trem-
bling for life and property ; all are in fearful expectation of the
events of a night in which even the efforts of despair are not
likely to afford the least resource to any individual. The
sole object of the domiciliary visits, it is pretended, is to search
for arms, yet the barriers are shut, and guarded with the
strictest vigilance, and boats are stationed on the river, at
regular distances, filled with armed men. Every one sup-
poses himself to be informed against. Everywhere persons

what to do with her miserable prisoner, he being extremely ill with a nervous fever, as they feared these visits, they were obliged to wrap him in a blanket and put him down a very dirty place, whence they could only take him out when the streets and houses were quiet. In short, she contrived to hide him till the 2nd

---

and property are put into concealment. Everywhere are heard the interrupted sounds of the muffled hammer, with cautious knock, completing the hiding-place. Roofs, garrets, sinks, chimneys—all are just the same to fear, incapable of calculating any risk. One man squeezed up behind the wainscot, which had been nailed back on him, seems to form a part of the wall; another is suffocated with fear and heat between two mattresses; a third, rolled up in a cask, loses all sense of existence by the tension of his sinews. Apprehension is stronger than power. Men tremble, but they do not shed tears: the heart shivers, the eye is dull, and the breast contracted. Women, on this occasion, display prodigies of tenderness and intrepidity. It was by them that most of the men were concealed. It was one o'clock in the morning when the domiciliary visits began. Patrols, consisting of sixty pikemen, were in every street. The nocturnal tumult of so many armed men; the incessant knocks to make people open their doors; the crash of those which were burst off their hinges; and the continual uproar and revelling which took place throughout the night in all the public-houses, formed a picture which will never be effaced from my memory.—*Peltier.*

September, when an order came out that every
section was to make visits at different hours of
the night in every house, and that the search
was to be very severe. It then became impossible for her to keep Monsieur de Chansenets
any longer. She knew that I had not been in
Paris since the 10th of August, and she therefore wrote me the note which I have already
mentioned, requesting me to come to Paris.

CHAPTER IV.

The Princess Lamballe's Murder—Incidents in the Escape of the Marquis de Chansenets—My Adventures in aiding him—Domestic Spies—Terror during Domiciliary Visit—Interview and Conversation with the Duke of Orleans—The Duke procures the escape of the Marquis to England.

I HAVE already given an account of the surprise of the soldiers on my entering Paris at such a moment of general consternation. On my road to Mrs. Meyler's, I met the mob on the Boulevard, with the head and body of the unfortunate Princess de Lamballe, which they had just brought from La Force, where they had murdered her; and in coming from thence they had had the barbarity to take it to the Temple, to show the poor Queen. At that moment, indeed, I wished that I had not come into Paris. On reaching my friend's house, I was much surprised to find that it was

G

poor Chansenets about whom she had interested
herself. I had seen a great deal of him before
the Revolution, at the Duke of Orleans', but I
had no very particular friendship for him.
He was now in such a weak state that he
could hardly support himself. I was very much
affected to see him in such a situation at such
a moment. I thought by getting him out of
Paris that night, which I imagined might very
easily be done, he would have a good chance
of escaping from the Jacobins. It was seven
o'clock when I arrived at my friend's house. It
was still too light to venture into the streets in
an open cabriolet with this poor man. I therefore waited until it was quite dark. We then
went directly to the Barrier de Vaugirard, which
was our way out of Paris. I made not the least
doubt that on showing my passport we should
get out of Paris directly. I was, however,
shocked and thunderstruck to find that they
refused to let us pass, though I assured them
that I had no sort of residence in Paris, nor
did I know where to go. I entreated them,
for God's sake, to let me go home; but all

to no purpose. Their orders were such, that they told me I should not be able to get out of any barrier in Paris; and they advised me to go and get myself a bed, or I should be taken up as soon as it was ten o'clock, for at that hour the domiciliary visits were to begin, when no carriages were allowed to be in the streets.

The sad situation of both Chansenets and myself at this moment may easily be believed. He was almost dead with alarm, and my knees were knocking together; and what added to my distress was the heat of the night. I ordered our driver to turn back. He asked me where he was to go? I didn't know what to say: I was afraid of raising the suspicion of the guards, who were not so civil as those of the morning. I did not dare go to my own home with Chansenets, as all my servants knew him, and I had a Jacobin cook whom I could not trust. Indeed I had not been in my house since the 10th of August, and my servants would have been surprised to see me arrive there at such an hour with a man. I therefore did not dare to think of my own

house, in company with poor Chansenets.   I
accordingly ordered the man to drive to the
Barrier de l'Enfer, as I could have got thence to
Meudon.   I was as little successful there, however; and as Chansenets never spoke, I began
to fear that our conductor would suspect us.   I
ordered him to drive to the Allées des Invalides,
on the Boulevards, as I thought of my friend
the gardener, though with little hopes.   It was
now ten o'clock, and I was much afraid that we
should meet the patrols.   Luckily we arrived
at the place where we were to take leave of our
cabriolet friend.   I could hardly get out, being
in such a tremble; but I cannot express what
my feelings of alarm were when I saw him
supporting Chansenets, and he not able to
stand.   I pretended to be in a great passion,
and told the man that my servant was drunk.
He said that he was sorry for it, but that he
must go home, as he had no mind to be taken
up for us.   Accordingly he drove off; and
Chansenets and I sat down for two minutes at
the foot of one of the trees.   The air soon re-
vived him a little, and he was able to stand.

I expected every moment that we should be taken up; and had that been the case we had not long to live, for we had little mercy to expect. We turned up an avenue which led to my gardener's house, but at this moment we saw, with horror, the troops at the further end of the avenue, and patrols coming our way. Monsieur Chansenets had been very ill ever since his fever; and being unable to support him, from weakness and agitation, arising from the certainty of our dangerous situation, I burst into tears. He, poor man, then entreated me to give him up to the first patrol, and by that means save my own life; as he said he saw with horror the cruel situation into which he had brought me, and that we had now no chance of being saved.

This idea was terrible to me. Had the scaffold been then before me, I could not have abandoned him, or anybody else in a similar situation. I soon began to feel more courage, and we turned round and crossed the Pont Neuf at the Palais Bourbon, and got to the Champs Elysées. We were fortunate enough

to avoid two patrols. When, however, we got
there, I was as much at a loss as ever. What
was to become of us? It was nearly eleven
o'clock, and none but soldiers were to be seen
about the streets. We could not remain long
unnoticed where we were. I was very near
my own house, which I could see from the
Champs Elysées; but I could not risk going
there with my unfortunate companion. I might
as well have given him up to the soldiers,
as expose him to my cook. I could have
depended on my own maid and porter, but I did
not dare. I was much fatigued; and Chansenets was fainting. He once more entreated
me to give him up, and to go to my comfortable home. This I assured him I would never
do; that since I had undertaken to save him,
I would do it, or perish with him.

Chansenets then asked me if I thought we
could by any means get to the Duke of Orleans' house at Monceau, and hide ourselves in
the garden, Monceau being now inside the
walls of Paris, and not far from the spot
where we then were. He thought that no

domiciliary visits would be made there; that
if the Duke knew it, he would say nothing on
my account; and he thought he remembered
a place where we might get in without
being seen. I did not like this plan, as I
had known nothing of the Duke for some
time, nor did I know where he was, and I
always feared his servants; but this was our
last and only resource.

I could hardly get to Monceau by a private
road without passing my own door, and cross-
ing the fields. When we came to the end
of the Rue Miroménil, where I lived, and of
which one end went into the fields, and the
other into the Champs Elysées, we saw my
servants sitting out at the gates, and amongst
them my Jacobin cook. I was much alarmed
at seeing this. However, there was a build-
ing near my house not yet finished, and I
persuaded Monsieur de Chansenets to go
into it, whilst I went to my own house to
see what I could do. He did so; and I
went up by myself to my servants, who were
much alarmed at seeing me come thither alone

and on foot, at so late an hour, nearly twelve
o'clock at night, when they thought that I was
in the country.   I told them that I had heard
at Meudon of the horrors which were going on
in Paris; that I could not rest in the country; and that I had taken a cabriolet, which
brought me to the barriers, and that I had
walked from there.   They related to me all the
murders which had been committed, and I sent
for my cook into the room and told her that I
had eaten nothing all day, that I was faint
with hunger, and that if it cost ten louis I
must have a roast fowl and salad. .She assured
me that nobody was allowed to go into the
streets, that she should be taken up, and that
nobody would sell anything at such an hour.
I told her that she must try, or I should
turn her out of my house the next day. Just
as she was going out of the room Monsieur
Chansenets knocked at my gates. He had
been frightened by seeing the patrols coming
into the street, and hardly knew what he was
doing.   On his entering my room both myself
and servants screamed.   I pretended not to

have seen him before, and asked him how he could think of coming to my house at such an hour, and in such a dreadful moment. He understood me, and said that he had been before the mayor, had been examined and acquitted; that they had given him leave to go to his own house, which was at Monceau, near that of the Duke of Orleans. My cook told him that the scaffold had been ready all day for him, and that a reward was offered to take him, but that she would not do him any harm then, though she knew that he was a nasty aristocrat; and she wondered at his coming to my house to expose me, and put them all in danger of being taken up as conspirators.

I pretended to be very angry, and Chansenets said that he would go directly. The cook then went out, as I ordered her, and I was left with my porter and his wife, my own servant being from home, as she was afraid that one of her sons was murdered. My porter, who was present, told me that I could not get out of the street to go to the Duke's, for the domiciliary visits had begun. In this dilemma we did not

know what to do with this poor man. My cook
I had managed to get rid of, but she might
soon return. . Monsieur Chansenets was almost
in fits, and in a deplorable state from ex-
treme weakness : in short, he could not support himself. My porter thought that he
might be hid between the mattresses of my
bed, which were very large, and in an alcove.
We accordingly pulled two of the mattresses
out further than the others, and made a space
next the wall, and put him in. When he
was there, we found that the bed looked
tumbled, and of course suspicious. I then
decided upon getting into bed myself, which
prevented any appearance of a person being
hid. I had all my curtains festooned up ; my
chandeliers and candelabra lighted, which in
all formed about twenty candles, as bed-rooms
in France are much ornamented. My cook
soon came home, and I made her sit by my
bedside the rest of the night. She abused
Monsieur Chansenets, and said that she was
sure he would be guillotined ; that she hoped
I had turned him out directly : in short, she

had not the most distant idea of his being in my house.

My own attendant now came home from visiting her son. She was a good woman, and as faithful as possible, yet as she had not been there when Chansenets was hid, I thought that it was better not to tell her anything about it till after the domiciliary visit had been made. I had some warm negus by my bedside, and when my maid and the cook went out of the room to see what was going on, I could just get at Chansenets to give him a teaspoonful of it. Indeed, I was frightened to death, for I heard him breathe hard, and thought that he was dying, and I expected every minute that my cook would hear him. In short, I passed a most miserable night, surrounded by my servants, and almost in fits myself at the idea of the horrid visit I was going to receive. I trembled so much, that I could hardly keep in bed, and the unfortunate man, who was the cause of my misery, I thought perhaps lay dead near me, for I could not hear him breathe at times.

At a quarter before four o'clock my cook

hurried into my room, telling me that the guards had arrived in my court, and that the municipal officers were coming in. No pen or words can give the smallest idea of my feelings at that moment. I felt that I was lost, nor did I know where I was; but a very deep groan from my companion roused me in a moment, and God inspired me with more courage than I had ever felt in my life. So strong was my abhorrence of the horrid acts which were being committed, that I am certain I could have mounted the scaffold with pleasure. Had the guards come into my room at that moment, I might have lost both myself and Chansenets, for I was determined to brave every danger, and to give myself up to them. Fortunately they visited every part of my house before they came into my room, and pulled my maid's bed and all the servants' beds to pieces, running their bayonets into the mattresses and feather-beds, swearing that they would not leave the house till they had found Chansenets. My maid and my cook, not knowing that he was in the house, were very bold and feared nothing; but the men said that he was seen to go into the house, and not go out.

This long search gave me time to cool, and to consider my deplorable situation. Although my own life was of little value, still I had no reason to suppose that the unfortunate man near me did not value his. I therefore thought that I had no right to commit any act of desperation, as the life of a fellow-creature depended on my conduct. These were, in truth, my reflections when the ruffians burst with violence and horrid imprecations into my room. I was then perfectly calm, full of presence of mind, and indeed inspired with a courage equal to anything earthly. The candles were all a-light, day was breaking, and my room looked more like a ball-room than a scene of the horrors which were passing. They came all up to my bed, and asked me to get up. One of them, however, less hard than the others, said that there was no occasion to take me out of bed, as I could not dress before so many men. They were above forty. I said directly that I would get up with pleasure if they required me to do so, but that I had passed a very cruel night, and was tired of my bed. I had expected them, I said, at an earlier hour, and then had hoped to pass the rest of the night in quiet. I owned that I had been much alarmed at the idea of such a visit in the dead of the night, but that now I saw how considerate, kind, and good they were, I was not the least alarmed, and that if they pleased I would get up and conduct them about my house myself. I added, that I was sure they must be much fatigued, and proposed wine or liqueurs and cold pie to them.

Some of the head men were delighted with me, cut some very indecent jokes, said that nobody they had seen the whole night had been half so civil; that they were sorry they had not come sooner, in order that I might have had a good night when they were gone. They would not now make me get up, but were obliged to go on with their visit, and must search everywhere in my bed and under my bed. They, however, only felt the top of my bed and at its feet, and then under the bed. They also undid all the sofa cushions, both in my room and into my boudoir and drawing-room, looked in my bathing-room; and, in short, were an hour in and out of my room. I expected every moment that they would again search the bed, as some of them grumbled, and said that I should get up, and that they had information of Chansenets being in my house. I said that they knew my cook, and might ask her in what manner I had received him when he came, and that I made him leave the house directly. She assured them of the truth of this, and that she was certain I would not have harboured so great a foe of the Duke of Orleans. They said that we should have given him up to justice, and have sent to them to take him up, as it would have made their fortunes. I replied, though I disliked him, yet I did not like to denounce anybody. They declared that I was then a bad citoyenne, and wished to know where they could find him. I told them that he said he was going home. They replied that they did not believe he would do that ; but that if he was in Paris they would find him in twenty-four hours. They then came back to my bed, and one of them sat down on it.

It may easily be supposed in what a state of alarm poor Chansenets was during this long visit. I had heard nothing of him, nor heard him breathe. At last the monsters advised me to take some rest, and wished me good night. They stayed some time longer in my house, during which time I was afraid of moving. At last I heard the gates shut, and my servants came into my room and told me that they were all gone. I went into violent hysterics, and was very much frightened. When I recovered a little I desired my cook and other servants to leave the room and go to bed, saying that I would take something, and go to rest myself. I directed my maid to bolt my room-doors, and then I disclosed to her what I had done, and who was in the bed. She screamed with dread when she heard it, and said that she never could have gone through the visit had she known it.

We now got our prisoner out of the bed with great difficulty, for when he heard the guards come into the room he had tried to keep in his breath as much as possible, and having been so smothered he was as wet as if he had been in a bath, and speechless. We laid him on the ground, opened the windows, and my maid made him drink a large glass of brandy. At last he came to himself, was full of gratitude to me—had been both frightened and surprised at my courage when the men were in the room, and the more so when I offered to get out of bed.

I was very ill myself from the agitation I had been in for the last four-and-twenty hours. We contrived to make the bed in my boudoir for our guest, but were obliged to be very cautious for fear of my cook, as none of my servants had gone to bed at so late an hour. We locked him in the room, and my maid took the key. I then went to bed, but had no rest, and rang my bell at two o'clock; I was almost dead with agitation. However, I got up, and my maid went into our prisoner's room. She

H

found him in a high fever and almost delirious, and crying; in short, he was in a most dreadful state. We were distracted, for fear of a discovery: had he died, where could we have put him, or what could we have done?

We were considering all this, when the Duke of Orleans came in. He was going to his house at Monceau, and seeing my gates open, had asked if I was in town. He was struck at my ill looks and seeming distress, and was anxious to know the cause of it. I told him the same story I had told my servants the night before, and then related to him the very horrid visit I had had in the night, and how much alarmed I had been. He assured me that if I had nobody hid in my house there was no need to have alarmed myself so much; but if I had, I certainly was in a dangerous situation. I told him that I had not been fortunate enough to save anybody in the dreadful night; that I wished that it had been in my power to do it even at the risk of my own life; that I thought the scenes of yesterday and this night were horrible; and I hoped they would cure all the admirers of the abominable Revolution.

The Duke replied that "they were indeed dreadful, but that in all revolutions much blood had been spilt, and that no stop could be put to it when once begun." He told me of the horrid murder of Madame de Lamballe—of their bringing her head to the Palais Royal whilst he was at dinner. He seemed much shocked at her fate, and said he had done everything in his power to save her. From what I afterwards heard I am certain that this was true, for at all times I heard him express great affection for this unfortunate Princess. He stayed some time with me, was in very low spirits, said that "revolutions ought to be of great use, and better our children, for they were very dreadful for those who witnessed and felt them."

I said that "I wished he had remained in England when he was there." He replied that "he should have liked it, but that they would not let him stay there; that they taxed him with having left France through fear of

H 2

Lafayette, and of his having attempted the King's life." He added that "nothing could have kept him longer out of France when he heard such reports. By his presence he would show the world he had no fear of Lafayette; that he had always been cruelly used by the Court; that when he did anything with good intentions, they imputed it to a bad motive. He assured me he had always envied the life of an English country gentleman; and that though his enemies taxed him with wishing to be king, he would willingly change his lot and all his fortune for a small estate in England, and the privileges of that delightful country, which he hoped to see once more." He asked me if "I thought him monster enough to be going through the streets of Paris on such a day as yesterday and to-day, and not feel unhappy."

I then entreated him to get out of the hands of the vile people who surrounded him, and not to let wretches make use of his name to commit such horrid acts.

He replied "All this seems easy to do in

your drawing-room : I wish that I could find
it as easy, but I am in the torrent, and must
rise or fall with it. I am no longer master
of myself or of my name, and you can be
no judge of my situation, which is, I assure
you, not a pleasant one. Don't plague me any
more ; don't talk in this style to your servants,
nor indeed to anybody else. We are all surrounded by spies, and if you get yourself into
a scrape I cannot save you ; so, for God's sake,
keep your politics to yourself, and plague me
no more on this subject ; it will be of no use."

I was half inclined to tell him about Chansenets, but I would not do it till I heard from
him whether he thought it safe, as the Duke
disliked him much, and thought that he had
been ungrateful to him after the Revolution,
for the Duke had given him (Chansenets) one
of his own regiments, though the Queen had
begged it of the Duke for somebody else, and
she was extremely angry about it. Indeed, no
regiment of a prince of the blood had ever been
given to a man of the same sort of rank as
Chansenets ; they were always given to the old

noblesse. When the Revolution broke out, Chansenets certainly behaved ill to the Duke, and had much displeased him. I was therefore more cautious of telling him on that account, though I knew he might with safety be trusted without the least fear of his making an ill use of the confidence.

The Duke said he " was sorry that I had come into Paris; that he feared I should not get out of it for some days, as the barriers were ordered to be kept shut whilst the visits were being made in search of conspirators." I was distressed to hear this, being at a loss to know how to keep my unfortunate prisoner longer in my house in Paris, so many spies were about me. Besides, they might again make me a midnight visit. I therefore entreated the Duke to try through his interest to get me a passport; but he assured me that " he had not interest enough to get one, and thought that as I had been foolish enough to come into Paris at such a moment, I had better stay quietly in my own house, and see nobody, and then go back to Meudon as soon as the barriers were opened.

By pursuing this course nobody would take notice of me, but that if I seemed so eager to leave Paris, they might suspect something."

He told me that the person who had the management of the barriers was Robespierre, a man whom he hated, and who hated the English. The Duke then took leave of me, after staying about three hours. He assured me that he " would see me next morning before he went to the Convention, where he was obliged to be at twelve o'clock." He said he thought I was looking very ill, and wished me much to see his physician, whose name was Seffert. I refused however to see him.

As soon as the Duke had left my house, I sent my maid into our prisoner's room, where he had been during the Duke's visit in great distress, having heard every word which passed. He said that he wondered " I had not told the truth ; that he seemed well-disposed and good-natured ; and that perhaps had he known the dangerous situation I was in with him in my house, he would have found some means of getting me out of Paris by the town-wall, some part of which is in his gardens." I assured Chansenets that I had only deceived the Duke from not thinking it fair to divulge a secret of such importance without first having his consent; but as the Duke was coming the next morning I would then tell him the exact story. He said that he wished the Duke would see him; for he could vindicate himself respecting his seeming ingratitude,—as never being able to leave the King, and being governor of the Tuileries, it had been out of his power to pay the Duke the proper attention he wished to do.

The next morning, September the 4th, the Duke came to breakfast with me before eleven o'clock. He was very low-spirited. I enquired of him if any new horrors were going on? He said that " he knew nothing; that he was just come from Monceau; but that he should hear news at the Convention."

I said that " I hoped the Royal Family were well, and that they were well used in the horrid Temple."

He replied that " he believed and hoped that

they were; though he was sure that they would not be sorry for him, if he was in a worse situation."

I asked him " how they could keep the poor King and his innocent family in confinement?"

He said, " Because when he was at liberty he was ill surrounded, and broke his word and oath to the nation."

I then told the Duke in as quiet a manner as I could what I had done. He seemed much surprised, and assured me that " I should be found out; that I was in great danger; and that most certainly if Chansenets did not get by some means or other out of Paris, he would be taken, and that both he and I would be executed."

I then entreated him either to get Chansenets out of Paris, or to suffer him to be hid in his house at Monceau. The Duke assured me that "such a plan was impossible; that all his servants were spies from the Jacobin Club; and that the part of the town-wall to which I alluded was surrounded by troops; in short, that he saw no means of his getting away."

He added that he was distressed and sorry for the scrape I had got into; that I must be cautious, and trust nobody with the secret, but contrive to conceal him till the barriers were opened, and then get rid of him as fast as I could, though he really saw little chance of my being in any safety.

He asked me " where I concealed him?" I said " in the roof of my house," as I did not wish the Duke to know that he had heard our conversation. He told me that " I had exposed my life for a very bad purpose, for that Chansenets was a good-for-nothing creature; that many better people had been taken up and executed; that he wished I had saved anybody else; and that it would be cruel if I was to lose my life for such a poor miserable being."

I was sorry that Chansenets should hear all this; however, I could not help it. The Duke inquired of me " whether Chansenets knew that he was to be let into this secret." I assured the Duke that I had told him by Chansenets' own desire; that he would give the world to see the Duke; that he could explain his conduct; and that he hoped and trusted for pardon, and that the Duke would put him in the way of saving his life.

The Duke said that " it would be impossible; that it would be very imprudent in him to see Chansenets; for that some of my servants would know it." I assured him that he might see him without any creature knowing it but my maid, who he was aware was much attached to both himself and me. He did not seem to like it, and then looking at his watch, said that " he must go directly to the Convention; that he was then nearly an hour too late; that he left me with regret in such a dangerous situation; wished I had been more prudent; that he would see what he could do to get this man out of my house, but entreated me to keep my politics to myself. He wished to God I was safe in England, for he thought something would happen to me here." On leaving he promised to see me the next day, and I ventured to say, " And pray see Chansenets." He answered, " *Nous verrons cela.*"

When I went in to Chansenets I found him as ill as possible. The manner in which the Duke had talked of him had alarmed him to a great degree, and he thought that he was gone to get him taken up. I assured him that he had nothing to fear on that ground; that I thought the Duke would see him, and try to do something for him the next day.

My maid was in Chansenets' room all the rest of the day and the evening, trying to console him. We were obliged to give him ether: at every knock he heard at the gates he thought it was the guards. When my servants were gone to bed, I went into his room, and told him that he had better make up his mind to see the Duke next morning, and desired him to be in my room when the Duke came in, as the Duke would then not fear his being seen; that my own maid would 'watch the Duke's coming, and would announce him. With great difficulty he consented, observing that as his life was in my hands I might use it as I pleased.

Chansenets then came into my room, and

about ten minutes afterwards the Duke arrived. He started at seeing Chansenets, to whom he bowed, and desired him to sit down. Poor Chansenets trembled so much that he could hardly stand. The Duke perceived this, and turned to me, and talked of my health. I was making tea, and when I had given the Duke his dish, he turned to Chansenets and said, " *Cela ne vaut rien pour vous.* You have been confined long and seem ill and weak; a bouillon would be better." Chansenets then said, "Monseigneur, you are all goodness. I have appeared very ungrateful to you: I wish to explain to your Highness why."

The Duke replied very gravely, " Monsieur de Chansenets, no explanations. We will neither talk of the past, nor on any other subject; but the situation of this good person who is trying to save your life at the expense of her own. She is ill, and I fear both you and she are in a scrape. I would be of use to you on her account if I could, but I fear that it is impossible. You and I must forget that we ever met before, as we never can again be in the same room; and

I never wish to hear your name pronounced in my presence. My opinion of you has been fixed for some time. I am sorry that you cannot get away, as I shall not be at peace till I see you out of her house." He then talked on indifferent subjects—no politics of any kind. At last he looked at his watch, and went away.

I did not see him the next day, but I heard from him. In short, I kept Chansenets in my house, without any of my servants or my Jacobin cook knowing it, till the barriers were opened. The moment that was the case I took him to Meudon, which was a bad place for him, as he was also governor of the castle of Meudon, and well known to all the people about there. But my house stood quite alone, and except an old lady and gentleman, who were my only near neighbours, and who were staunch royalists, nobody but my maid knew that he was at Meudon, though the searches for him were still being continued in Paris, till somebody said that they saw him lying amongst the dead on the 10th of August. This I fancy cooled their further searching.

I had more uneasiness, for I heard from the Duke that visits were going to be made at Meudon. At this time he sent me one of his old valets-de-chambre, who was a royalist, to deliver me a letter from him, telling me that the mail-cart which stopped at St. Denis, would, for fifty louis, take Chansenets to Boulogne, from whence he might soon get to England. The Duke also sent me a note for the master of the inn at St. Denis, called the *Pavillon Royal.* I did not tell Chansenets whence this information came, for he would have been alarmed, and would not have gone; but I assured him that Meudon was dangerous, and that I could now get him to Boulogne.

We accordingly went in a cabriolet, my old royalist neighbour and myself, to St. Denis, at three o'clock in the morning. The mail-cart came in an hour afterwards. We settled with the man, giving him his fifty louis, and I saw poor Chansenets, in a deplorable condition and much disguised, set off. There were other emigrants in the cart also. It was in January, and quite dark.

Some years afterwards I heard that Chansenets got safely to England, even before, I believe, the unfortunate King's death. After Chansenets' departure everything got worse and worse, and on the 21st of January the Parisians murdered their innocent King.

CHAPTER V.

The Murder of Louis XVI—The Duke of Orleans promises not to vote—Visit of the Duke of Orleans and the Duc de Biron to me—Conversation relative to the death of the King—The Duke of Orleans breaks his solemn promise—Anecdote of an attached Servant of the King—General Terror—My Illness; the Duke sends to me—Anxious to get away to England—The Duke unable to assist me—I upbraid him for his conduct in voting for the King's Death—His Defence—The Countess de Perigord's horror for her situation; begs my aid to get away—Monsieur de Malesherbes — Another Domiciliary Visit — Madame de Perigord concealed in a Closet—Melancholy position of the Duke of Orleans—I am arrested.

IT was at this time that the Republicans began to talk of bringing the unfortunate King to trial; but the idea seemed so monstrous and infamous, that people could never imagine it possible they would dare to attempt such an act. However, everybody knows that

I

that horrid crime was committed before the face of all France, and that the monsters carried their audacity and vengeance to the last extremity by bringing the most virtuous and best of kings to the scaffold, like a common criminal.

I must here mention my unfortunate friend the Duke of Orleans, over whose conduct from that period I could wish to throw a veil, for nothing earthly can excuse it; the more so as he had pledged himself to me in the most solemn manner that nothing should induce him to vote, unless it should be for the King's deliverance.

Some days before the final decision as to the King's fate, the Duc de Biron called on me in the morning, and said that he was come to have his fortune told. I used often to fool and play with the cards, and pretended to tell fortunes. He was extremely superstitious, and really thought that I had told him some truths before he went to the army. I assured him that " I wished both the Duke of Orleans and he had believed more firmly the things I told them; for then the King would still have retained his crown, and they would have been surrounded with pleasure and comforts, instead of lurking about without daring to have a house or a carriage to cover their heads. I told him moreover that the King's trial was the most abominable, cruel event ever heard of, and that I wondered some brave Chevalier Français did not go and set fire to the house in which the Convention sat, and burn the monsters who were in it, and try to deliver the King and Queen from the Temple. He told me that he felt unhappy at the King's trial, but that the worst which could happen to him would be seclusion till things were settled; that certainly some would vote for his death; but what gave him great comfort was, to be sure that the Duke of Orleans would not vote, as he had told him so.

I had never then mentioned this subject to the Duke, therefore I told the Duc de Biron that I wished the Duke of Orleans would vote for the King's deliverance. He assured me that he never would do that; that we must content ourselves by his not voting at all; as he feared, that if the King was sent out of France, he would engage the Powers to invade France, and that the Duke and all his friends would then be lost.

I assured him that I would sooner see even such an event, than that the Duke of Orleans should disgrace himself by voting for the seclusion of the King, little then imagining what would happen. The Duc de Biron said that he should like to meet the Duke of Orleans the next day at my house, as when he saw him at Madame de Buffon's he was always surrounded, and as he was to come in the course of the day, I appointed that it should be at two o'clock.

It was on a Thursday, the 17th of January, 1793, that they both came. I had seen little of the Duke of Orleans for some time before. On my asking him what he now thought of the wicked trial which was going on, and saying "that I hoped he did not go near such vile miscreants?" He replied that "he was obliged to go, as he was a deputy." I said,

From an Original Miniature.   J. Brown sc.

LOUIS JOSEPH PHILIPPE, DUKE OF ORLEANS.

London Richard Bentley 1858

"How can you sit and see your King and cousin brought before a set of blackguards, and that they should dare to insult him by asking him questions?" adding that "I wished I had been at the Convention; for I should have pulled off both my shoes, and have thrown them at the head of the President and of Santerre, for daring to insult their King and master."

I was very warm on the subject. The Duke of Orleans seemed out of humour. The Duc de Biron then asked him some questions about the trial. I 'could not help saying, "I hope, Monseigneur, that you will vote for the King's deliverance?" "Certainly," he answered, "and for my own death."

I saw that he was angry, and the Duc de Biron said, "The Duke will not vote. The King has used him very ill all his life; but he is his cousin, therefore he will feign illness and stay at home on Saturday, the day of the *Appel Nominal,* which is to decide on the King's fate."

I said, "Then, Monseigneur, I am sure you

will not go to the Convention on Saturday.
Pray don't."

He said that he certainly would not go; •
that he never had intended to go; and he gave
me his sacred word of honour that he would
not go; that "though he thought the King
had been guilty by forfeiting his word to the
nation, yet nothing should induce him, being
his relation, to vote against him." This I
thought a poor consolation, but I could do
no more, and the two dukes left me.

I saw nobody on the Friday. Every one
seemed anxious for the termination of this
abominable trial, though few expected that it
would end as it did. How could any creature,
indeed, dare imagine that such a crime was
hanging over France?

On the Saturday I received a note from the
Duc de Biron to beg me to come and pass the
evening with him and Madame Laurent and
Dumouriez, at the Hôtel St. Marc, Rue St.
Marc, near the Rue de Richelieu; that there I
should hear the news, and that he had great
hopes things would be softened. At this time

the Duc de Biron had no house or home;
he had been denounced to the army by one
of the revolutionary generals called Rossignol,
who was a murderer of the 2nd of September. The Duc de Biron, who was then
called General Biron, had come to Paris at this
period to exculpate himself with the War
Minister, and he lodged during the short time
he was there at this *hôtel garnie*.

I went there at about half-past seven
o'clock, and found the Duc de Biron and the
party there assembled very dismal. He had
every half-hour a list sent him of the votes,
and we all saw with agony that many had
voted for the King's death. He also heard
that, at eight o'clock, the Duke of Orleans had
entered the Convention, which surprised us all.
I feared much that he was going to vote for
the seclusion, for I never thought of worse.
However, every list was more and more alarm-
ing, till at about ten o'clock the sad and fatal
list arrived with the King's condemnation, and
with the Duke of Orleans' dishonour.

I never felt such horror for anybody in my

life as I did at that moment at the Duke's conduct. We were all in deep affliction and tears; even poor Biron, who, alas! was a republican, was almost in a fit. A young man, who was the Duke's aide-de-camp, tore off his coat and flung it into the fire, saying that he should blush ever to wear it again. His name was Rutaux, and he was a native of Nancy. He was a noble, and a very good young man, who had not emigrated out of affection for poor Biron, though his heart was always with the Princes. When my carriage came, I went home; but every place now seemed dreary and bloody to me. My servants all looked horror-struck. I did not dare sleep in my room alone. I desired my maid to watch with me all night, and we kept up a great light and prayed. I could not sleep. The image of the innocent King was constantly before me. I don't think that it was possible to have felt even a family calamity more than I did the King's death. Till that moment I had always flattered myself that the Duke of Orleans was misled, and saw things in a wrong light; now, however, all that illusion was over. I even threw the things he had given me which I had in my pockets and in my room out of it, not daring to stay near anything that had been his.

Such at that moment was the vexation that I felt about a person for whom some time before I would have given my life. Nobody can have an idea of my sufferings; but, indeed, every honest person in Paris felt, I believe, as much as I did.

The next day, Sunday, I heard that the fish-women were to go in a body to the Convention, or to the Hôtel de Ville, to insist on the King's deliverance, as he was to be executed on the Monday. However, the monsters caused a proclamation to be read in the streets, declaring that if any women were found abroad on the Monday they would be outlawed, and might be fired on.

I now determined not to remain in Paris another hour, and getting a passport from my Section, I went with my own maid to my house at Meudon, that I might not breathe the same air as the King's murderers.

On the 21st, Monday morning, I hoped every instant to hear that the Parisians had risen, and delivered the King. Just at ten o'clock I heard a cannon go off.   This I hoped was some tumult in the King's favour; but, alas! that was the moment when his august head fell!

Meudon is on a mountain, and with a glass I could have seen the Place Louis Quinze, where this horrid murder was committed.   I went out on the mountain to try and meet with somebody who had come from Paris, and who could tell me the King's fate.   At last, about twelve o'clock I observed a man coming along the road, with a handkerchief in his hand steeped in blood.   I knew the man: he had been one of the King's workmen, belonging to the Palace of Meudon, and much attached to his royal master.   He related to me the dreadful event.   He had gone, he said, to Paris, in hopes of being of use, had any attempt been made to rescue the King.   He was under the scaffold, and pulled the handkerchief off his neck, dipping it in the King's

blood as " a relic of St. Louis the Sixteenth."
These were the man's own words. He gave me
a small bit of it, and died about two months
afterwards of grief, with the bloody handkerchief on his heart. Several of the game-
keepers of the park of Meudon, who used
to go a-shooting with the King, also died of
grief.

The King was shooting at Meudon on the
5th October, when the mob went to force him
to go to Paris. This was the last amusement
which his Majesty took.

The day of the King's death was the most
dreary day I ever saw. The clouds even
seemed to mourn. Nobody dared appear, or at
least look at each other. The cruel Jacobins
themselves seemed to fear each other's reproach.
I was shut up all day. I heard nothing from
Paris, nor did I wish to hear. I dreaded the
idea of ever going there again.

From that period everything bespoke terror.
Robespierre became all powerful. People did
not dare to speak above their breath. Two
people, the most intimate, would not have dared

to stop and speak.   In short, even in your own rooms you felt frightened.   If you laughed, you were accused of joy at some bad news the republic had had; if you cried, they said that you regretted their success.   In short, they were sending soldiers every hour to search houses for papers of conspiracies.   These soldiers generally robbed people, or made them give them money, threatening them in case of refusal to denounce them.

I wished to remain quiet at Meudon, but was soon found out, and never having been in favour with the republicans, they annoyed me in every way possible.   They denounced me at the Jacobin club at Sèvres; said that I had hid Chansenets, and other emigrants; that I had flour hid in my house; and that I had entered into a conspiracy to get the Queen out of the Temple.   In short, I hardly ever slept a night undisturbed by visits from the municipalities, not of Meudon, for they were kind to me, but of Sèvres and of Versailles, which were horrid. About six weeks after the King's death I was taken very ill, and was obliged to send to Paris for a physician. He was a Dr. Leroy, who had been one of the Court physicians.

The doctor had mentioned in Paris my being extremely ill; in consequence of which the Duke of Orleans sent an old and faithful valet-de-chambre of his, (who was a good royalist) to see me, with a very affectionate letter regretting that "he did not dare to come to me, but entreating me to see him when I was well, saying that all the world had given him up, and that he thought his unhappy situation would have made me forgive him, if I thought he had done wrong." In short, the Duke sent every day from Paris to Meudon to inquire after my health, and was kind and attentive to me. As at that moment I wished to get a passport to return to England, and thought that nobody could get me one but him, I fixed a day to go to him at the Palais Royal, intending to return to the country at night. Accordingly I went, and found the Duke's antechamber full of officers and generals; in short quite a levée. Romain, the Duke's good old valet-de-chambre, took me up to what was called *les petits appartemens.* I was very much affected and agitated at the idea of seeing the Duke, as I had not seen him since he gave that horrid vote. Romain and I wept much both of us at the idea of the Duke's present situation. The poor old man loved the Duke like his own child, and had been in his service since the day the Duke was born at St. Cloud. He little expected ever to see him what he then was.

The Duke came up when I had been there about an hour waiting. He was dressed in deep mourning, looked embarrassed and very grave. I was nearly fainting, and he made me sit down, and himself gave me a glass of water. "You look ill," he said, "but I hope you are quite recovered from your cold?" I told him that his black coat made me remember terrible events, and that I supposed he was, as I was, in mourning for the King. On this he forced a smile; and said, "Oh, no; I am in mourning for my father-in-law the Duc de Penthièvre."

"I suppose," I said, " that the King's death has hastened his; or perhaps the manner of his cruel trial, and your having voted for death ?" Here I burst out into tears, and said, " I dare say that he died broken-hearted, and so shall I ; but you, Monseigneur, will die, like the poor King, on the scaffold."

" Good God !" said he, " what a situation you are in ! I am sure I should not have made you come here, had I had an idea of all this. The King has been tried, and he is no more. I could not prevent his death." I then replied, " But you promised that you would not vote."

On this he got up, observing, " This is an unpleasant subject. You cannot—must not judge for me. I know my own situation. I could not avoid doing what I have done. I am perhaps more to be pitied than you can form an idea of. I am more a slave of faction than anybody in France ; but from this instant let us drop the subject. Things are at their worst. I wish you were safe in England, but how to get you out of France is what I cannot contrive. If money can procure you a passport I will give five hundred pounds. This is my last resource for you. The rulers like money, and

I have hopes for you. I will do what I can with
some of the leaders, but Robespierre, to whom
I never speak, is all powerful."

The Duke wished me to make breakfast, and I
drank some tea, but felt so very uncomfortable
that I could say nothing to him, but about
the horrors of the Revolution, a subject which
did not seem to please him.   He asked me if
"I was going back to the country to dinner?"
I told him that I was going to dine at my
own house, and to order fires to be lighted for
some days; that I should not stay at Meudon,
because the Sections of Versailles and Sèvres
used me very ill. He said that if that was the
case, I had better come to Paris, though he
feared that the Section in which I lived was
also very bad, and would plague me.   He told
me that people said I had been very imprudent
during the Revolution; and he entreated me
not to talk or tell people what I thought, or
to say that I was in mourning for the King;
adding, "If you like to wear mourning for
him, in God's name wear it, but say that it is
for some of your relations, or you will get into

a scrape, and I should never be able to get you out of it. I wish that you could have remained in the country, till you could obtain a passport for England. I wish that *I* had never left it, but now I can never see it again."

I then took leave of the Duke, and went to my house in the Fauxbourg St. Honoré, telling them that I should return to Paris on the Sunday following, which I did.

I passed over the Place Louis Quinze on my road home to Meudon, and felt a shivering all over when I saw the spot where the unfortunate King's head had fallen. Paris was then indeed dreary; no carriages were to be seen in the streets but mine and two or three more. Everybody seemed afraid. No visits were paid or received. The playhouses were filled with none but Jacobins and the lowest set of common women. The deputies were in all the best boxes, with infamous women in red caps and dressed as figures of Liberty. In short, Paris was a scene of filth and riot, and the honest, sober part of the inhabitants were afraid of

K

being seen or even dressed with common decency.

When I returned to Meudon, I found a note from Madame la Comtesse de Perigord, wife to Archambeau de Perigord, to say that she should take it as a great favour if I would see her; that she was much harassed; and that she had no hopes but in me, in whom she had the greatest confidence. I have her letter now before me. I wrote to her and appointed her to come to me on the Monday following at my house in Paris. When I saw her, she told me that she was the most miserable woman on earth; that her Section had found out that her husband had been hid in Paris; and that she did not know what would become of her and her children. She thought that I might be able to get her, through the Duke of Orleans, the means of making her escape. She said that she wished to go to England; and that her aunt, Madame de Sennason, and her uncle, the venerable and virtuous Malesherbes, were miserable about her situation. She declared that she was terror-stricken; that she must and would fly, or destroy herself, for she could exist no longer. She said that being so very rich, they certainly would murder her; that she had jewels and some ready money, and that she would try to get to England, where her husband and eldest son then were. She went down on her knees to me, begging me to see and entreat the Duke of Orleans to assist her; for she thought him all-powerful. I informed her what he had told me about my passport. She then was in despair; rolled herself on my carpet, and I really feared that she had lost her senses.

She stayed with me some time; and when it was dark I, with my own maid, conducted her to her aunt Madame de Sennason's house at the Porte St. Honoré, which was not far from me; and there I had the happiness of sitting two hours with the poor King's friend Monsieur de Malesherbes, and of hearing from himself an account of his last interview with the unfortunate Monarch. I was even blessed by Monsieur de Malesherbes, and he pressed me to his breast, praying God to bless me, and protect me! Poor man, I never saw him again!

He was too good to be spared long by Robespierre, though he was long in prison.

I now sent to the Duke of Orleans requesting him to come to me the next day about my passport. He replied to me by telling me that "I must not now think of it; that he had done everything in his power, but had been desired by a person in power to advise me not to ask for it, or talk of England at that moment, but to bear my misfortunes like other people, and to keep very quiet." The Duke desired me to give Madame de Perigord the same advice; but she would not take it, and indeed she lost herself by not following that advice. The Countess de Jarnac called on me that same afternoon, and told me that she came from Madame de Perigord, who was at her house, which was near mine, quite distracted, and determined to get out of Paris at all events, and that she would see me, but Madame de Jarnac had prevented her coming, for fear that she should expose herself to my servants. I returned with her to her house, and there we found Madame de Perigord, who was determined not to sleep in Paris that night, even if she slept in the fields.

I forgot to mention that a domiciliary visit was to be made that night, which had frightened her. She entreated me to take her and her children, a boy and a girl (now Madame Juste de Noailles), to my house at Meudon, only for that night. I had an old woman there who kept my house while I was away, and on whom I could depend. Ordering my carriage, therefore, directly, I, Madame de Perigord, and the children went to Meudon, where I left her as comfortable as was possible at such a moment. As the people of my Section knew that I was in Paris, they might have suspected something had I gone away and not slept in my own house, the more so as there was to be a domiciliary visit. During that visit I was not at all frightened. I had then got used to it, and had nobody hid in my bed; therefore I was not very civil to the intruders. I had promised Madame de Perigord to go to her the next day. Madame de Jarnac told me, that if Madame de Perigord would come back to Paris, a person whom she knew was going to Calais, and would manage, with a false passport, to get her there. I did not approve of this scheme; but I brought Madame de Perigord and her children back to Paris, and kept her and them in my house for ten days or more.

This was, I think, in March, near the time when Dumouriez went out of France, accompanied by the Duke de Chartres, son of the Duke of Orleans. The Duke de Chartres, on his emigration, wrote his father a most harsh letter, which his father never forgave till the day of his death. His son upbraided him much with the King's death; I perfectly remember the letter, for I had it two days in my possession. The Duke burnt it in my room, the last time in his life that he came to my house. On this occasion he came accompanied by two gensd'armes in his coach. I was much shocked and surprised to see him in such a situation, but he laughed, saying that it was only because his son, the Duke de Chartres, had gone off with Dumouriez, and that he owed that obligation to him. The guards stayed in my antechamber. The Duke asked me if I would give him a breakfast on the Sunday, when he hoped to come with less suite. I said that I would. He observed that as nothing now was certain, and that as his fate was more uncertain than that of anybody else, he did not feel at his ease about the money I possessed, which I had placed on his estates. He thought, in case of his death, he could make an arrangement for me which would secure the payment of my annuities in England; that he would arrange all the business and give me effects, which would be money to me when I could get to England. He assured me that I should be far from being a loser, and that if they paid his creditors after his death so much the better, for I should then be so much the richer. I own that it gave me pain to hear him talk so, as, indeed, I expected his fall every day.

He then went away. Madame de Perigord was in my house all this time; but she slept in my own maid's room up-stairs. She and I were sitting by the fire, talking about what had just passed, when my maid bounced into the room and said, "*Madame, une visite des gardes!*" Madame de Perigord had only time to get into a closet, where we had before taken the shelves out for that purpose, when forty men came into my room. They stated that they came to inspect all my papers; and that I must give them my keys. It was twelve o'clock at night. I was frightened lest my friend should cough; but knew that the men could not find the closet, as it was between the two doors, and covered with paper, so that there was no keyhole, and the person who was in it could fasten the door on the inside.

I assisted them to search my papers; and those which were English they packed up. At last they found a sealed letter, directed to Charles Fox. Sir Godfrey Webster, who was then at Naples, had sent it to me by a French courier who came to Paris from Admiral Latouche Freville, who had been before Naples to make a manifesto in the name of the French nation. I knew very little of Sir Godfrey Webster; but he thought that I could get this letter sent to England.   The people who made the visit to my house were ignorant men, who had heard of Mr. Pitt and Mr. Fox, but did not know anything of their politics.   They thought that I should be sent the next day to the guillotine; and they were enchanted at the discovery they had made.   They told me that they had long suspected me, but that now they had found out that I was in correspondence with the enemies of the Republic, and that I should pay dearly for it.   I assured them that Mr. Fox was their friend; that he was in correspondence with the Comité de Surveillance, which was then their great tribunal.   They stated that they had orders to put me under arrest that night; and they put their écharpes over their shoulders, and arrested me in the name of the République Française. They took all the papers they pleased, and hardly allowed me time to put a shawl over my shoulders, though it was very cold; and put the seals on my cabinets.

It may easily be conceived what poor Madame de Perigord must have suffered during

this night.   She thought that they would have
put the seals on my room-doors ; and, though
my maid was to remain in my house, yet it
was death to break a seal put on by them.   It
happened, however, that they were so pleased
at getting me out of my own house, and lead-
ing me, as they thought, to the scaffold, that
they left my house without seals.   On the
next day I heard, with pleasure, that Madame
de Perigord got safely that night to Madame
de Jarnac's.

CHAPTER VI.

Taken to the Guard-room, where I pass the night—Walked between Soldiers to the Mairie to be examined—The Duchesse de Grammont and the Duchesse du Chatelet before the Mairie also—Their miserable Fate—Frightful Scenes at the Feuillants—Encounter the Duke of Orleans there—My examination and alarm — Brutality of Chabot, the Capuchin—Civility of Vergniaud—Letter of Sir Godfrey Webster—I am allowed to depart, but stopped by Chabot —The Duke of Orleans arrested, with the Comte de Beaujolais—Affecting Scene between the Duc de Biron and the Comte de Montpensier—The Duc de Biron sent to St. Pelagie—Madame de Perigord leaves her Children with me —I am sent to St. Pelagie—Meet Madame Du Barri—Her Violence at her Execution—Fatal Letter of Mr. Vernon—I am released.

IT was two o'clock when we entered the guard-room where they took me. The soldiers were lying asleep about the room; some drunk, others drinking, smoking, and swearing. There were some other miserable prisoners like myself, none of whom I knew; nor was there any other woman in the place. They gave me a seat on a bench near the fire, and offered me wine, saying, that I must not be proud ; that there were now no more dukes or princes ; that they were all good citizens ; and that if I had not been a conspirator I should have been a good and happy citoyenne ; but that I was now going to dance the Carmagnole in the Place Louis Quinze.   I assured them that I was in no fear of that ; for if they had nothing to accuse me of but that letter to Mr. Fox, I was sure of being acquitted.   I told them that I wished they would break the seal and read the letter, for they would then find that it was not a letter to a foe of liberty, but to a great patriot ; and that they might break open the letter, though I would not and could not, as it was merely sent to me to try and get it to England.

I remained the whole night in this miserable place, without anything but the bare walls to lean my back against. They took no further notice of me during the night. About six o'clock in the morning, my maid and one of my men-servants brought me a basin of tea and some bread, my house being in the next street to the section-house. I was fatigued to death, and had a violent headache from the constant smell of wine and tobacco I had been exposed to all night. The members of the *Comité Révolutionnaire* of my Section, who had come to my house with the guards to arrest me, were various tradesmen, and the president was a barber, who had been a zealous actor in the prisons on the 2nd of September, and of course was a monster. When they had conducted me to the Corps de Garde, they went home to their beds, and left me with the soldiers.

About eight o'clock in the morning they all returned to conduct me to the *Mairie*, where the state prisoners were examined. This place was close to the *Palais de Justice*, which was at the further end of what is called the *Cité*, on the other side of the water from where I lived. They had the cruelty to make me walk in the middle of the soldiers, and the streets were dirty. When we got there we found the room full of prisoners, like myself, waiting their

turn to be examined. I am sure that there
were at least two hundred—a great many
women, and most of them of high rank.
During the whole time I was there, which was
thirty hours, I was close to the poor Duchesse
de Grammont and the Duchesse du Chatelet. I
believe that there were not ten chairs in the
room, and the women were fainting from fatigue.
The Duchesse de Grammont was very bulky,
and her legs were terribly swollen.

A young aide-de-camp of the Commander
of Paris, whose sister used to wash my laces,
saw me, and pressed through the crowd to give
me a chair. Seeing Madame de Grammont
and Madame du Chatelet, who were older than
myself, I was, of course, happy to offer it to
them. They made many compliments about
taking it, and Madame de Grammont said,
" Pray, madame, tell me who you are, that if
ever we get out of this place we may meet
again, for I see that you are also persecuted for
the good cause." I told her ; and she was good
enough to assure me, that she was enchanted to
have an opportunity of seeing a person who

had been so staunch to the cause, and who had rendered it such services. She knew all that I had done for Chansenets, and for her cousin, Madame de Perigord. The Abbé de Damas had often told her, she said, of all I had done, and that she had long known the good advice I had given to an unfortunate Prince. She hoped to God that the monsters would spare me long, as she was sure that I still might be of use to the unfortunate. In short, from nine o'clock in the morning of Friday till twelve o'clock on Saturday morning, did I again remain on my legs, except for about five minutes now and then when these ladies pulled me on their knees, but I was so much afraid of hurting them that it was no ease to me.

There was a *buffet* at the end of the room where we could have anything to eat or drink we liked, on paying for it; but few who were there thought much of nourishment. Their situation was too dangerous, and they had very little hopes of ever again returning to their own houses. By talking in a low voice we could say anything, for the room was too full even to have guards in it; so they were stationed at the different doors. I saw many people whom I knew, and many gentlemen and ladies of high rank, but I was not so near them as I was to the two old countesses. They both perished some time afterwards on the scaffold. They were imprisoned at Porte Royale, and I was at the Carmes. Madame de Grammont was examined about four o'clock in the morning, and they treated her harshly, but let her return to her own house again for some time. They did the same to Madame du Chatelet. At twelve o'clock on Saturday they took me to the mayor, I think his name was Chambronne. He went in the coach with the King when he was murdered. When the people of my Section told him of the cause of my arrest, and showed him the letter, he said that he could say nothing to me; that my case must go before the Comité of Surveillance, then sitting at the Feuillants, near the Convention; and that mine was a grave business.

I then was marched again in the same manner back to the Feuillants, in the Tuileries gardens, where I saw, while I waited, most dreadful scenes—poor men and women coming out of the Comité in tears; papers having been found upon them ; every one whom I saw was ordered for imprisonment, and to be tried by the horrid *Tribunal Révolutionnaire*. I really felt alarmed at my own situation, as I had no idea what the contents of Sir Godfrey Webster's letter to Mr. Fox might be, nor had I any idea of his politics. They did not keep me long, however, as they had been in a private comité for some time examining a prisoner. When the door opened, who should come out, attended by guards, but the Duke of Orleans! He saw me, and seemed hurt. "Mon Dieu!" said he, "are you here ? I am very sorry indeed."

He then went out, and one of my guards told me that the Duke got into his coach, but did not go to prison.

When I went into this awful room, the members, who were Vergniaud, Guadet, Osselin, and Chabot the Capuchin, all sat along a green table, and a chair was placed facing them. There were at least forty present. I have only named

L

those I can remember. The chair was very high up steps. I felt much frightened as I mounted the steps. They began by asking the people of my Section what was my crime, and why I had been arrested? They then told the story and produced the letter. Chabot asked me what were the contents of the letter? I assured him that I was ignorant of them; at which Chabot said, "It is a conspiracy. I know this woman; she is a royalist. She has been intriguing in England to make D'Orléans' daughter marry an English prince. Send her to La Force."

Vergniaud, who was civil, said, "I don't see why this woman should have been arrested, because a letter directed to Mr. Fox was found in her house. Had it been directed to the monster Pitt, you could have done no more. Mr. Fox is our friend; he is the friend of a free nation; he loves our Revolution, and we have it here, under his own hand-writing; therefore can we with honour break open and read a private letter directed to that great man? No! it shall not be; we will keep the letter, and send it safely to Mr. Fox."

They began to be very warm, and Chabot insisted on the letter being opened and read. Osselin accordingly opened it, and they found that it was in English. As they had no interpreter they were much at a loss, as he was gone to examine some English papers in the Fauxbourg St. Germain. Osselin, who was president, made me leave the chair, and come to his side and read the letter and interpret it to them. They said that some of them understood English enough to know whether I told them the truth.

In the first place, Sir Godfrey Webster had enclosed in this letter a printed paper in French, which was Latouche Freville's manifesto to the King of Naples. I then proceeded to read his letter to Fox. It was full of praise and admiration of the courage and energy of the French nation, and also of high admiration of the manifesto. In short, the letter greatly delighted them.

As the interpreter came in, and read it as I

had done, they were all in good humour with me except Chabot.   Osselin wanted to conduct me home in one of the coaches belonging to the Comité, for they had all coaches.   This I declined.   I told them of the two cruel nights I had passed, and they were very angry with the people of my Section.   However, I noticed Chabot in conversation with the barber; and when I was about to leave the room, and Osselin was giving me his arm, Chabot said softly, "Citoyenne, I have some more questions to ask you.   Do you know D'Orléans or *Egalité?*"   I said, "Yes."   "Had you not some conversation with him in the outer room before you came in here?"   I said, "I merely asked him, how are you?"   "And pray what did he say?"   I told them that he said "Mon Dieu!   I am sorry to see you here indeed!" Chabot said, "Then it is plain that he thought and feared that you were to be examined on his account, and that he was alarmed lest you should betray him."

I now became very much alarmed and hurt, and burst into tears.   He said, " We don't mind tears. I wish that we had all those which had been shed in this room—they would supply all the houses in Paris with water." He then went on, "Don't you know that D'Orléans wanted to be king, and destroy the republic?" I said, " I am sure that he never did." He said, " You know that he did: he voted for the King's death for that purpose." I said, " I wish from my soul that he never had done so ; he might now be happy." " Why then did he do it?" " Because you all forced him to commit that dreadful sin." " So you think that it was a sin? You are very impudent to say so here ; for we are fifty members in this room, and we all voted the death of the tyrant Capet, but not to be kings ourselves, but only to rid the world of that horrid race. And now we will see what we can do for this would-be-king, who was always turning to that gulf of liberty, England, where he is now in corre-spondence, and so are you. I shall not let you escape. Send her to La Force ; she must go to the Tribunal ; let us settle this."

About twenty of the members then got up,

and said that this was not right; that they must take more information respecting me; that I should have leave to return home; that if I was a friend of Fox, I could not be a conspirator. In short, they were in a dreadful uproar about me, when Robespierre came into the room. He seemed much occupied about some event of importance, and I was dismissed till further orders.

I returned home and went to bed, though it was not more than four o'clock. At eight o'clock the Duke of Orleans sent to my house, to say that he would come and see me the next day, Sunday, at twelve o'clock. When I woke they gave me his note. I answered it, and begged that he would not come, as I wanted to go to Meudon early in the morning; but that I should return at night, and should be glad to see him. I told my servant to take it to the Palais Royal at eight o'clock in the morning. My servant returned directly afterwards, and brought me back my note. He informed me that the Duke had been arrested in his bed at four o'clock in the morning, and taken without servants or anybody but his son the Comte de Beaujolais, a boy of eleven years of age, to the prison of the Abbaye; and that his servants were gone to the Comité of Surveillance to try and get leave to attend him there. They allowed him his valet-de-chambre, Mongot, for that day, and a footman for the child.

This event much shocked me, as the end was now too plain. Mongot came to me on the Monday about two o'clock, and told me that they had kept him all night in a cell, and that at three o'clock he heard a carriage with post-horses drive out of the prison-yard. He suspected that it was the Duke whom they were carrying away, as they had confined him. About ten o'clock in the morning they set him at liberty, and told him that his master was gone where he never could see him again. They had been to the Palais Royal to get his travelling-carriage at twelve o'clock the night before. He had eight post-horses and sixty gensd'armes to escort him to Marseilles, for it was there they took him and the little Comte de Beaujolais.

They confined them in the Fort St. Jean, quite at the bottom, where he, I understood, was very ill-used. I never saw him afterwards. When he was brought back to Paris to be tried and executed, I was myself a miserable prisoner.

Monsieur le Duc de Montpensier was then at Nice, aide-de-camp to the Duc de Biron, who commanded that army. An order had been sent directing poor Biron to arrest the young Prince, and to send him with a strong escort to the Fort of Marseilles. This was a cruel task for him to perform against the son of his old friend, and against a young man whom he loved as his own child. They were just going to sit down to dinner at the moment when the order came. The Duc de Biron was so much affected when he saw the order that he shed tears, turned pale, and could of course eat no dinner. He looked very sadly at the Duc de Montpensier, and the young man flew to him, saying, " General, is my poor father murdered? you look at me so mournfully, and are so much affected. I am sure it is true.

Tell me, in the name of God, the worst!" The Duke then took the young Prince in his arms, and showed him the cruel order. In great joy, he said, "Is that all? Good God! how my mind is eased! I thought that my father was no more. Let me go directly; I shall try to amuse him in his captivity."

This anecdote the Duc de Biron told me soon afterwards, when we were both prisoners in St. Pelagie.

About ten days after the Duke of Orleans had been sent to Marseilles, the Duc de Biron was sent to St. Pelagie from Nice, under an escort. He never left that prison till he went to the *Tribunal Révolutionnaire,* and thence to the scaffold. He suffered death about ten days after the Duke of Orleans.

On the Monday morning on which the Duke was sent to Marseilles, Madame de Perigord came to me with her son and daughter Melanie, the latter about nine years old. She is now Madame de Noailles. Her son was about five years old. Madame de Perigord told me that she was going off in the night with a friend of Madame de Jarnac for Calais; and that her aunt, and her uncle, Monsieur de Malesherbes, had been arrested that morning. She declared that she would not stay, but would leave her two children in France ; that she had brought them to me, as I was the only person in the world to whom she would intrust them. She entreated me to adopt them as my own. She then put the two children in my arms, and we had a very affecting scene. She soon afterwards took her last leave of them and me, and returned to Madame de Jarnac, whence she went to Calais.

Six weeks after having these dear children under my protection, I was sitting hearing Melanie read, when the members of the *Comité Révolutionnaire* of my Section came into my room, and told me that now I really was going in good earnest to prison, and they visited my papers, putting the seals all over my house. Without their hearing me, I ordered my maid to take the children as soon as I was gone to Madame de Jarnac, who had been desired by their mother, in case of my arrest, to send them to a person who had been her maid.

After they had made the visit of my papers, and ate some dinner, which I, of course, did not, they allowed me to take linen and everything I wanted, put me into a hackney-coach, and drove to the prison of St. Pelagie, a most deplorable, dirty, uncomfortable hole.   This prison had been used before the Revolution as a house of correction. It was six o'clock when I got there in the month of May.   It had been a beautiful day, but no appearance of spring or summer was to be found in this sad habitation !   The other prisoners were, like myself, all in tears, dreading what was to happen, and full of pity and kindness for me, their new companion. We became all intimate friends in a moment. There I saw many who I had hoped were out of France ; but about eight o'clock, when they brought us our miserable supper, ham, eggs, and dirty water, whom should I see, and who should come and take me in his arms, and burst into tears, but the unfortunate Duc de Biron ! I scarcely ever was more affected in my life.

In the prison also I found Madame Laurent, a friend of the poor Duke's. Of course the prisoners were eager to hear the news, as they had no sort of intercourse with people out of prison. I could only wound them with horrible truths of what was going on. The next day many other prisoners arrived, and every day more and more. Many were daily taken off to the scaffold. I feared for poor Biron. We could have little conversation, for the men and women were on different sides in that prison; indeed our chief conversation was from one window to the other opposite.

I did not stay at St. Pelagie long. It was in June, I think, that I left it; but cannot be exact, as the months were different in France, and I never really knew what month it was. Poor Madame Du Barri came there before I left it. She was very unhappy. She used to sit on my bed for hours, telling me anecdotes of Louis XV. and the Court. She talked to me much of England and of the Prince of Wales, with whom she was enchanted. She regretted much ever having left England. She dreaded her fate.

Indeed, she showed very little courage on the scaffold; yet, I believe, had every one made as much resistance as she did, Robespierre would not have dared to put so many to death, for Madame Du Barri's screams, they told me, frightened and alarmed the mob. She was very good-natured, and during the time I lived in the same prison with her I liked her much.

I had been sent to St. Pelagie while the *Comité du Salut Public* was visiting the Duke of Orleans' papers, and they thought that I should be found to have been an agent of the Duke's about England. They found, however, nothing that could induce them to suppose that I had any correspondence with the Duke; and I was fortunate enough to have been sent for by the *Comité du alut Public* to hear a letter read in English, which was found on the visit of the Duke's papers. They wanted to learn if I knew anything of the writer, who he was, and what it could mean? I was much alarmed when the guard took me from St. Pelagie to the Tuileries, where the Comité sat. However, I found that this famous letter to the Duke was one from old Mr. Vernon about horses and bets, and Newmarket, &c., all of which they thought had a double meaning. In short, that unfortunate letter was once more produced at the Tribunal on the poor Duke's trial, and was one of the pretexts for condemning him to death.

They kept me all night under examination, but they found that I could give them no great satisfaction. In the morning they sent me home, and people to take the seals off my house. I never knew why they treated me so well at that moment. While I was at the Comité they received a letter from the Duke of Orleans to desire them to send him *soixante mille francs*, and I heard them say that *trente mille* was enough for his expenses. The members who examined me were Barrère, Billaud de Varennes, Merlin de Douay, and Robespierre, who asked me himself several questions, but he was not at the Board: he was going in and out of the room. All this took place in the King's fine room in the *Pavillon de Flora*, where they held the Comité;

and the same furniture remained which the poor King had. It was in that very room that all the murders were signed, even that of the unfortunate Queen herself.

I went from St. Pelagie without supposing that I was not to return, and therefore took no leave of my poor friends there. My own house was very dreary. I never was one moment happy; at every noise expecting that they were coming to arrest me. I almost wished that they had left me in St. Pelagie. I had no friends. The only person whom I saw now and then was Madame de Jarnac. She, poor woman! was not in better situation than myself. I also saw Mrs. Meyler. She came to live in my neighbourhood.

CHAPTER VII.

My Flight on being warned that I am to be arrested—
Incidents of my Flight—Reach Meudon—I am pursued and
sent to the Prison of the Recollets, at Versailles—Brutality
of the Section—A Condemned Jew—Dr. Gem imprisoned
in the same room with me—Our miserable Food—I procure
the discharge of Dr. Gem—Deprived of everything—And
pray for Death—Brutality of Gaoler—Young Samson, the
Executioner—The Queen's Death.

ABOUT the 6th of September I went one
night to see Mrs. Meyler, who was ill. With
her were two or three French ladies, and
we supped together. I was in better spirits
than for some time previously. About half-
past eleven o'clock, I walked home with
my servant. This was a late hour at that
period in Paris. When I came into my room
to undress, my maid looked very dull, and
she said, "Mon Dieu! Madame, how gay you

look to-night! I have not seen you look so gay or so well these many, many months."

"No," I said; "I really feel myself more comfortable than I have done this long time."

She wished, she said, that I might have nothing to damp my ·mirth; adding, "God forbid, that I should!"

I said, "Then don't look so dismal. I hate to see you look so!"

She asked me if I had heard anything of the Queen's trial? I was sorry she talked of that, for it made me unhappy. At that moment the trial of the unfortunate Queen was going on. I then went to bed. My maid wished me "good night," two or three times, and kissed my hands. I felt her tears on my hands. I soon fell asleep, and about six o'clock in the morning my maid came into my room, and said, "Madame, get up directly. There is no time to lose. You are to be arrested at nine o'clock; and your death-warrant is signed! I had this information last night from your grocer, who is one of the members of the Section, but he wishes you well, and advises you

M

to make your escape. I was to have told you this last night, but I had not the heart to do so ; you looked so happy, and I have not seen you so for a long time."

I only half-dressed myself. I took my diamonds, and other things which might be put into my pocket. I did not even wait to tie my petticoats on, for we did not for certain know when the wretches might come. I ran into the fields behind Monceau, but did not know where to go. All the morning I wandered about the new Boulevards, till I got to the Porte St. Denis. Then remembering that Milor, the maître-de-ballet of the Opera, and his wife, Bigotini, lived at the top of the Fauxbourg St. Denis, although I hardly knew them, I went there, as they were staunch royalists, and were known to be good people. They received me with kindness, pitied me, but could not keep me, as they expected visits in the night, and I should be searched for. They therefore thought it best for me to try and get to my house at Meudon, when it was dark. M. Milor was good enough to walk with me there at ten o'clock at night, and to return in a cabriolet, which he was fortunate enough to meet with at twelve o'clock at night.

I then went down with my dairy-maid to the village, and made the mayor get up. He was an honest labourer, who had a great regard for me, as had many others of the same class, who belonged to the municipality. I told the mayor my situation; that I expected every hour the people from Paris would arrive to arrest me; that of course when they could not find me in Paris, they would be sure to come there. I told him that all I feared was being taken to Paris; that the people of my Section had always ill-used me, and accused me of being a royalist; and that I should be lost if I were taken again to the prisons in Paris. I entreated him to call up the municipality and arrest me, and then keep me in the castle prison of Meudon.

The mayor, who was a very sensible man, said that he could not assist me; that Versailles was the chief authority for the Seine et

M 2

Oise; that I was then out of the department of Paris, which was that on Seine only, and that my Section could not touch me there. He assured me that if I would go home to bed, they would not come; that he would get on his horse and ride over to the *Comité Révolutionnaire* at Versailles; and that they should come and arrest me in the morning.

The members of Sèvres could have arrested me, but I dreaded them, as they were as bad as Paris for me, and always called me a royalist. I took the mayor's wife home with me, and she slept in the next room to me —at least for an hour, for we had hardly been longer in bed, when there came a most dreadful thundering and ringing at my gates. My gardener went and let them in. It was the Section from Paris, who had been for that of Sèvres, as Meudon was in the department of Seine et Oise, and they could not have taken me alone. They made me get up before them and the gensd'armes, who were all in my house. They searched my things; upbraided me for making my escape, and said,

"*Ah ! ma mignon, vous nous n'échapperez pas* this time. You will make a good appearance on the Place Louis Quinze. We will all go and see you make your exit : it will be quite a fine sight."

While they were sealing, and stealing half my clothes, the *Comité* of Versailles arrived. They were furious at those of Paris for having dared to come into their department. They also were very angry with those of Sèvres for joining them without the leave of those of Versailles. Both were for having me, and I anticipated that they were going to fight, had not the gensd'armes interposed. At last they sent a soldier on horseback to Versailles, to one of the deputies of the Convention, who was at the head of the department of Seine et Oise, to know what to do. He sent a written order that I should be delivered up that moment to the *Comité* of Versailles, and that I should be taken directly to the prison there called the Recollets. In short they kept me on my legs the whole day, and they drank and cooked their own dinner in my rooms, and stayed till nine o'clock at night.

From five o'clock in the morning it had been
and then was, a rainy, nasty day. I was put in
a cart with some wet straw, and the few things
which they allowed me to take, with two gens-
d'armes, four of them also following it. In this
way we went through the woods to the *Comité*
at Versailles, who sent me to the Recollets.

When we got to the prison, the gaoler said
that he had no place prepared for me, and that
I must stay all night in the guard-room of the
prison; as there was a bed there, and I might
lie down. I was wet to the skin, and ill with
weeping all day, and so tired that I could hardly
hold my head up. The gaoler's wife brought
me some warm wine and some cold beef and
salad. Of this I ate something, and drank the
wine, drying myself at the fire. The guards
who were in the room were very civil and
good. They said that they would not smoke
in the guard-room, but would go and sit out
on the stairs all night; and that I might
safely lie down and sleep, for they would allow
no creature to come into the room, or to insult
me. Accordingly I lay down with my damp

clothes on, and I slept till seven o'clock. I really believe that in the whole course of my life I never slept so soundly, though God knows that I was not happy; but complete misery had stupefied me.

In the morning I was taken into the prison, a dreary place; however, it was better than St. Pelagie. Here I found no prisoners but felons. I was placed in a very large room, which had been previously to my arrival occupied by about three or four hundred rabbits, and was offensive and dirty. I am sure that there was room for at least forty beds. In one corner was a miserable truckle-bed, with two old chairs and a dirty old table, a candle and candlestick, dogs and fire-irons, and a fire-place where an ox might have been roasted at full length. I had indeed an immensely large fire, which looked comfortable. For the whole time I stayed in that prison, I was never refused fire, as they were at that time burning all the gates and barriers, rails, and green posts which were in the woods and parks round Versailles.

I was now examined and visited by the deputy who was commanding in the department of Seine et Oise. He was the terror of everybody about there ; but I was fortunate enough not to displease him in the conversation we had, and ever after I found him inclined to treat me better than the other prisoners. I was much annoyed at having in the next room to me a poor Jew, who was condemned to be executed the following day, for having robbed and murdered a farmer at Rambouillet. He made a most terrible lamentation, and cried all night, which made me very unhappy. I talked to him early in the morning from my grated window, exhorting him to trust in God for pardon, and to suffer his punishment with resignation. I told him that I myself might soon be in a similar situation ; and that though I had committed no crime which merited death, yet I should not complain as he was doing. They brought the cart for him at eleven o'clock in the morning, and he confessed the crimes, and died very penitently.

This event, and my own cruel situation,

brought me into so nervous a state the whole day, that I knew nobody, nor did I even swallow a bit of bread, though I understood that as I had money in my pocket I might have anything I pleased to eat or drink. About eight o'clock in the evening, as I was sitting crying by my fire, the gaoler and his wife came into the room with a bed like mine. They were kind to me, and said that they were happy to tell me that I was going to have a companion. I asked, who? They said, a very old man, and that he was English. I was hurt at the idea of having a male companion.

However, when the poor prisoner came in, I found that it was old Dr. Gem, an English physician, who had been forty years in France, and who was eighty years of age. I was indeed much hurt to see a man of his great age entering such a wretched place. He was himself much shocked and surprised to see me there, as he had heard that my fate was soon to be decided. He knew that he ran no risk of being murdered; for he was a *philosopher*, and I am sorry to say an atheist. He seemed to want much to talk of these subjects to me; but I used to entreat him to leave me in what he called ignorance; for religion was my only comfort in all the trying, miserable scenes I went through. That alone supported me to the last, while he, poor man, was in despair at being shut out from the world and every comfort. I used to try and divert him, and make him laugh. He then would burst out into tears, and say, " You seem contented and happy, when you may probably in a few days be dying on the scaffold; while I, a miserable old man, am regretting a few paltry comforts." I used to make his bed and clean his part of the room, wash his face and hands, and mend his stockings; in short, do every office for him which his great age and weakness prevented him doing himself.

At that period we were allowed candles till ten o'clock, at which time the prison was shut up. My old friend used to go to bed at seven o'clock, but I remained up till ten o'clock at work. He used to get up at four o'clock and uncover the wood fire, and light a candle and read Locke and Helvetius till seven o'clock. Then he would come to my bedside, and awake me, and many a time has he woke me out of a pleasant dream of being in England, and with my friends, to find myself in a dreary prison expecting my death-warrant every time the door opened.

My old friend frightened me sometimes, as I feared that he might die in the night, and the gaoler lived at the end of the court. Besides, we were barred into our rooms with the felons next to us. When Battelier, that was the name of the deputy, came, I asked to have an audience of him. I told him before all the *Comité* of Versailles, who were there, that this poor old man might die suddenly, and asked that he might be transferred to some other prison, for that I had not strength enough to support so tall a man when he was in his fainting fits. I said, moreover, that it was cruel to leave me alone with him; and that they should allow his old housekeeper to come there and take care of him. As he was a Republican, I said, I could not conceive why they should not let him remain in his own house with a guard, whom he had no objection to pay.

The deputy said that he thought as I did; and that he should leave the prison the next day, and be confined at his house at Meudon. I never felt more pleasure than in having this good news to tell my old friend. After the audience I was conducted up to my own room, where I found the poor doctor in bed fast asleep. For a while I sat and watched him. He awoke about ten o'clock, and I then told him the good news. He was delighted to go home, but he really felt unhappy about me. I had procured him his liberty, but mine was only to be obtained on the scaffold! He wept much, and so did I at parting. He never expected to see me again; but, however, we did both live to meet again, and I saw him the day before he died. He had from the commencement of his imprisonment a great regard and affection for me; and when I came out of prison used to walk a mile to see me every day. This old gentleman, who was well known in the literary world by, I believe, some writings, was grand-uncle to Mr. Huskisson, Under-Secretary of State.

Once more I was alone, but only for a very short period. The Terror gained ground so fast, that the prison was soon filled with unfortunate royalists, and we were then deprived of every comfort. The little money which we had was taken from us, and our silver spoon and fork'; though, strange to say, I got mine back again two years afterwards, for when the gaolers took them from us they gave us a number, and told us that our things were sent with that number to the Hôtel de Ville.

When I got out of prison I was one day looking over some papers, and found my number, which was 79. My maid offered to go to the Hôtel de Ville with it, and see what they would say to her. On delivering in my number they gave her my spoon and fork out of many others, together with the money, thimble, scissors, knives, and other articles; at which we were much surprised.

We were now deprived, in short, of every comfort, for we were henceforth fed by the nation. The gaoler was allowed about eight pence English a day for our food, and God knows he did not spend six pence. We had for constant food boiled haricots, sometimes hot and sometimes cold; when hot they were dressed with rancid butter, when cold with common oil; we had also bad eggs dressed in different ways. A favourite thing was raw pickled herrings, of which they gave us quantities, as the Dutch had sent great quantities of them to Paris to pay part of a debt which they owed to the Republic. Sometimes we had what was called soup and bouilli, but we were always sick after eating it. Some of the prisoners thought that it was human flesh which was given us; but I really think that it was horses' or asses' flesh, or dead cows. In short, the poorest beggars in England would not eat the things which we were forced to do. Our bread was made of barley, and very dirty, and used to make our throats sore. At that time I had a very dangerous sore throat, and was not able to swallow the least thing for three days. I had no gargles, no softening things, or even a drop of clean water to cool my mouth, though I was in a raging fever. No creature who had not been in such a situation can imagine what I suffered. I prayed fervently for death. Though I was in a miserable dirty truckle-bed, yet I thought that anything was better than perishing by the hands of the executioner, and being made a show for the horrid crowds which followed the poor victims to the scaffold. However, without care or comfort I was miserable in finding that my throat got better, and at last I was restored to perfect health. While I was ill my unfortunate female companions were all kindness to me; they even deprived themselves of the little water they could spare for my use.

Common misfortune had made us sincere, even romantic friends, and we were always ready to die for one another. The gaoler used to fill for us in the morning a wine-bottle full of dirty water, and each prisoner had his own. That was to serve for the whole day, for the gaolers would not have been at the trouble to fill

them twice. Sometimes we used to get a drop
of brandy from the turnkeys, who had always a
great leather bottle in their pocket, and used to
offer us a drop out of it. However nasty, I
found it of great use to me, as I always washed
my mouth with it, and was one of the only
prisoners who had not tooth-ache, and who
indeed did not lose their teeth, from the damp-
ness of the rooms, which were very large. The
gaoler who was in that prison when I first
went there had been dismissed, and one of the
Septembrists was now put in his place. From
that period our life was a scene of agony.
Once or twice I asked the gaoler for a little
warm water to wash myself. This he told me
would be nonsense; for nothing could save
me from the executioner's hands, and as they
were dirty, it was no use to clean myself.

I was much shocked one day on going into
the gaoler's room, where we used sometimes to
go when we wanted anything. He was sitting
at a table with a very handsome, smart young
man, drinking wine. The gaoler told me
to sit down, and drink a glass too. I did

not dare to refuse.   The young man then said,
"Well, I must be off," and looked at his watch.
The gaoler replied, "No; your work will not
begin till twelve o'clock." I looked at the man,
and the gaoler said to me, "You must make
friends with this citizen; it is young Samson,
the executioner, and perhaps it may fall to his
lot to behead you."   I felt quite sick, especially
when he took hold of my throat saying, "It will
soon be off your neck, it is so long and small.
If I am to despatch you, it will be nothing
but a squeeze." He was going at that moment
to execute a poor Vendean prisoner in the
market-place of Versailles. We had many prisoners taken from our prison to Paris to be
tried by the *Tribunal Révolutionnaire,* who
were all executed. I was in hopes that I
should have remained long at Versailles.

About the 26th of October the news of the
poor Queen's execution reached us. Nothing
now surprised us; for we had then been used
to nothing but horrors. We heard of the
Queen's greatness and courage with admiration,
and we all determined to try and imitate so

N

great and good an example.   All envied her
her fate ; as indeed we did that of every victim
when their execution was over; but there was
something dreadful in being dragged through a
rabble to a scaffold.

CHAPTER VIII.

Death of the Duke of Orleans—Melancholy feelings on the Event—Nothing found among his Papers concerning me—Crasseau the Deputy—His Brutality to me—Imprisoned in the Queen's Stables—The Prisoners from Nantes—Conveyed to Paris—Insulted by the way—General Hoche—Madame Beauharnais—Madame Custine—The Marquis de Beauharnais is sent to the same Prison—Affecting parting between the Count de Custine and his Wife—The Reign of Terror—Santerre—I am released.

On the 5th of November I heard of the fate of the unfortunate Duke of Orleans. It is needless to say what I felt on that occasion. I was not aware that he had been removed from Marseilles to Paris till I heard of his death. I know that he died with great courage. He was tried, condemned, and executed in the space of two hours! A man-servant of mine by accident met the cart in which he was, in the Rue du Roule, near the Pont Neuf. He

knew that there were condemned people in it,
but he was shocked to death when he saw the
Duke of Orleans in it. .My poor servant was
nearly fainting, but was determined to follow
the Duke to the scaffold. There was very little
mob the whole way, though by the time they
got to the Palais Royal, the Duke's own palace,
people began to assemble. Till that moment
no creature had even an idea of the Duke's
having been tried. Under his own windows
they stopped him for ten minutes. He looked,
my servant since told me, very grave, and as
he did in former days when he was going out
on any occasion of ceremony. He was very
much powdered, and looked very well. His
hands were tied behind him, and his coat
thrown over his shoulders. His coat was light
grey, with a black collar. When the cart moved
from the Palais Royal, the Duke looked at the
mob with a sort of indignation. He did not
alter in any way, but carried his head very
high till the cart turned on the Place Louis
Quinze; then he saw the scaffold before him;
and my man said that he turned very pale, but

still held up his head. Three other prisoners
were with him in the cart—a Madame de Kolly,
a very beautiful woman, wife to a farmer-
general, a man of the name of Coustard, a
deputy of the Convention but of the Gironde
party, and a blacksmith of the name of Brouce,
for having made a key to save some papers.
It was nearly four o'clock when the cart got
to the scaffold, and it was almost dark. Therefore, in order that the mob might see the Duke's
head, he was the first who was executed. He
leaped up the ladder with great haste, looked
round at everybody, helped the executioner to
undo his neckcloth, and did not speak one
word or make the least resistance. They
afterwards held up his head to the mob.

Thus ended the life of a man who will never
be forgotten, and whose last crime will cause
his name ever to be remembered with horror!
I dare hardly say that he had many amiable
qualities, and that his horrible fate was brought
about by a set of ambitious men. As I have
previously observed, they left him in the hands
of men still worse than themselves. Unfortu-

nately the Court never allowed him a chance of getting out of their hands. I could say much on this subject; but I should not be believed, and the subject always makes me unhappy.

In the beginning of December, the poor Duc de Biron suffered death, nearly a month after the Duke of Orleans had been executed. I heard that he was much affected at his own situation, and showed some weakness in his last moments.

When the seals were taken off the Duke of Orleans' papers, which was soon after his death, I was closely confined in a dungeon, without even being allowed to converse with the other prisoners. I was very uneasy, fearing that the letter which I had written to the Duke after the King's death might have been found, and that alone would have condemned me. However, nothing of mine was found, and after three weeks' close confinement, and living with rats and mice, I was allowed to mix with the other prisoners. At that time a new deputy named Crasseau came to be at the head of the department of Versailles. He was a great friend of Robespierre's, and had great powers. He came to visit our prison, and said that I seemed to have too much *luxe*, and that I was very much perfumed, and therefore was sure that I was a royalist. I said, "I certainly was, or I should not now be in prison." He said, if I was "I should go and join my friends in the *Cimetière de la Magdalene*—that was the only place for royalists." I told him that I often wished myself there, or anywhere to be out of my misery. He said that he "should take care that my wishes should be soon accomplished;" adding that "it was indeed neglect in the other deputy not to have sent me up to the *Tribunal Révolutionnaire* before, but that he would have justice done, since I owned myself a royalist." I said, "Why, I am sure you never could doubt that, else I should not have been so cruelly used. I suppose you don't imprison the republicans. I am certain that if I had been ever so good a republican, I should have hated the Republic and have wished its destruction

a thousand times, for all the misery I had
suffered." On this he became furious. He said
that "I should go to Paris, and that I deserved
he should send me there that instant; that my
name was noted at the *Comité de Salut Public*; and that I should soon be brought to
the guillotine, for I had been one of the agents
of D'Orléans for England, and wanted either
to have made an English prince king of France,
or D'Orléans. He added that he knew "I had
had correspondence with the Prince of Wales;
and that I was only fit to be food for the
mouth of a cannon."

In short, three weeks after this I was once
more removed from this prison, to my great
grief and consternation; and taken at nine
o'clock at night, just as I was going to bed, to
the late Queen's stables, where many of the
poor people of Nantes had just arrived on
their road to Paris to be tried. They were in
a most miserable plight, having been marched
on foot from Nantes, many of them very ill;
some dying on the road, it is supposed of the
gaol distemper. This, however, I doubt, as I

slept on the same straw with them all night in the stables, and though they were full of vermin I got nothing dirty from them. This I impute to a sweet-scented sachet I always carried in my corset, which caused that monster Crasseau to say that I was covered with luxury.

The day after I left the Recollets for the Queen's stables, a cart covered over at the top like a waggon, with large iron bars at the end, was brought into the stable-yard. It was filled with straw, and we were put in, as many as it would hold. I understood that other carts arrived afterwards for the other prisoners, who were in all above forty, though I was the only prisoner from Versailles. Every one of them was taken to the Conciergerie but myself. I was taken to the Grue of Plessis, a terrible prison; but there was no room for me in it. On the next day therefore I was sent to the Carmes in the Rue de Vaugirard, a prison notorious for the horrid murders committed there on the poor old priests and the respectable and good Bishop of Arras.

I ought to mention that on our road from

Versailles to Paris, the populace of Sèvres pelted us through the bars of our waggon with mud, dead cats, and old shoes. They were very violent, and called us dogs and aristocrats. In short we met with ill-usage all the way. I regretted having left the Recollets; there at least the air was better than in Paris, and many good, respectable people were there, such as poor farmers and old labourers, who could not make up their minds to the Republic, and who had in their own villages expressed too freely their abhorrence of the new system. Many of these truly good and pious people were executed. There were some nobles in the prison also, but few of note. When I got to the Carmes I was very unwell and tired, very dirty and uncomfortable. At the greffier-room of the prison I found General Hoche, who had just been sent there. I had not known him before, nor had I ever till then sat down in a room with any republican officer, and I think that had I been at liberty nothing earthly could have made me make such an acquaintance. He, however, was very kind and civil to me. He had long, he said, known me by sight, and was sorry to make himself known to me in such a place.

I said, "General, if you know me, you cannot be surprised to see me here; but I assure you that I am much surprised to see you here, for I thought you one of the defenders of the Revolution." "So I am," said he, "but they seem to forget and oppress their real friends; however I hope that I shall not stay here long. I have been cruelly slandered." He asked me, who was in the prison? which I did not know, as the greffier had not done writing for at least two hours. They brought Hoche and me some dinner, very nasty. On account of our dismal situation we became afterwards very good friends. When we entered the prison, Hoche and I found many people whom we knew, and many great ladies, who all seemed to know him, such as the Duchess D'Aiguillon, Madame Lamotte, Madame Beauharnais, now Madame Bonaparte, Madame de Custine, and her husband, who was beheaded three days after I went into the Carmes. I knew there

also Madame de Jarnac, my friend Mrs. Meyler, and Madame de D'Araij. Before we went
to bed, we were all as good friends as if we had
been brought up together. Indeed, at every
instant we all equally expected our death-
warrant. They were delightful women, and
bore their misfortunes with courage and good
humour.

Most of the prisoners, like myself, had little
reason to hope they would leave the walls of the
Carmes, but for the scaffold ; yet in spite of this
horrid prospect, I must own that I passed many
pleasant moments with those very agreeable
women, who were all full of talent, none more
so than Madame Beauharnais, now Madame
Bonaparte. She is one of the most accomplished, good-humoured women I ever met with.
The only little disputes we had when together
were politics, she being what was called at the
beginning of the Revolution constitutional, but
she was not in the least a Jacobin, for nobody
suffered more by the Reign of Terror and by
Robespierre than she did.

When I first went into the Carmes I

slept in a room where we were eighteen
in number, and Madame Bonaparte, Madame
de Custine and I had our beds close together,
and we have often made our beds, and washed
the room, for the other prisoners did not take
much pains about it. Two old Frenchmen and
their wives slept in our room : they were nobles,
and virtuous, pious people. I ought to say that
in none of the prisons unmarried men were allowed to sleep on the same side of the house
with the women. Some who had their relations on the women's side, were permitted to
come to us for an hour or two.

Madame Beauharnais had been parted for
some years from her husband, the Marquis
Alexandre Beauharnais. We were therefore
much surprised one day to see him come into
our room, as a prisoner. His wife and he were
both much embarrassed at the circumstance,
but in a few hours they were perfectly recon-
ciled. A small closet with two beds, was
granted to them, where they slept together.
The day of Beauharnais's entrance into the
prison was a sad day for that beautiful little

creature Madame de Custine; for on that day her husband, a very handsome young man and son to General Comte de Custine, was taken out of our prison, tried, and beheaded the next day!

I never saw a scene of more misery than the parting between this young couple. I really thought that she would have dashed her brains out. Madame Beauharnais and I did not leave her for three days and nights. However, she was young, full of spirits, and a Frenchwoman, and at the end of six weeks she got into better spirits; so much so, indeed, that poor Madame Beauharnais, who really seemed to be attached to her husband, became very unhappy. I was her confidante, and did everything in my power to persuade Beauharnais to spare his wife's feelings, who had entertained a sincere friendship for Madame de Custine before this event. I am far from supposing that any improper connection was formed; but certainly Beauharnais was more in love than it is possible to describe; and the little woman seemed to have no objection to his attentions.

But, alas! this did not last long; for the Convention imagined, or pretended to imagine, that there was a conspiracy in our prison. We were all denounced by Barrère; and they asserted that we had laid a plan to set fire to the prison. In short, so cruel yet absurd was the accusation, that when the *Comité du Salut Public* sent for fifty prisoners out of our number to be tried for the conspiracy, the gaoler, who was a horrid Jacobin, laughed at the soldiers, and said, " A conspiracy! why the prisoners here are all as quiet as lambs." However, fifty were led out of our prison to the scaffold for that same conspiracy. Amongst the number, who were all men, was poor Beauharnais; the Chevalier de Chansenets, brother to him whose life I saved; the young Duke de Charost; the Prince of Salms; a General Ward, an Irishman in the French service, and his servant; and a young Englishman of the name of Harrop, who had been sent to the Irish college for his education, and whose parents had never sent for him home. He had been imprudent, and had abused the Republic in some coffee-house, in consequence of which he was arrested. He was only eighteen years old: Two other young men, in going down the prison-stairs, which were formed like a well, took hold of each other's hands, and leaped down. They were dashed to pieces; but as the number was to be fifty, they took two other people to make up the number.

I never saw such a scene as the parting of Beauharnais, his wife, and Madame de Custine. I myself was much affected at poor Beauharnais' fate, for I had known him many years. He was a great friend of the poor Duc de Biron, and I had passed weeks in the same house with him. He was a very pleasant man, though rather a coxcomb. He had much talent; and his drawings were beautiful. He took a very good likeness of me, which he gave poor little Custine when he left us. His poor wife was inconsolable for some time; but she was a Frenchwoman, and he had not been very attentive to her. The other lady I never saw smile after his death.

The whole fifty were executed the next day. They came into our ward to take leave of us.

I knew several of them, and poor Chansenets showed great courage, more than his poor brother did with me. I took leave of the Prince de Salms, but I did not pity him much; he had almost been a Jacobin. The Duc de Charost was a sort of madman; he was a descendant of the great Sully, and had married Mademoiselle de Sully, who was immensely rich. Hoche, who was at this period very closely confined in a dungeon, we never saw; but they allowed him at last to mix with the other prisoners, and he was then a great deal on our side. He was a very handsome young man, with a very military appearance, very good-humoured, and very gallant. His father had been body-coachman to Louis the Sixteenth, and he himself was brought up from an infant in the depôt of the French Guards. I believe that he was an excellent officer, at least I have heard Pichegru say so. Hoche was liberated before the death of Robespierre, and a command was given him. At the time he left the prison we had little hopes of escaping from the guillotine. Every day prisoners went from our

o

prison to that fatal end, and we were almost in despair.

A poor man and his wife, who used to keep a stall for puppets in the Champs Elysées, were brought to our prison for having shown a figure of Charlotte Corday, which was handsome. These poor people were honest, good creatures, and though we could do them no good, yet they used to render us every service in their power. We were in hopes, as they were poor, that they would have escaped; but, alas! they were dragged also to the terrible scaffold, and we all wept their loss sincerely. In short, the scenes became so dreadful, that it was impossible to exist much longer in such a state of constant woe, to see husbands forced from their wives' arms, children torn from their mothers, their screams and fits, people when they could get a knife even cutting their own throats! Such were the horrors going on in the Carmes, and we expecting, and indeed being told, that every day might be our last. This was what I believe we all wished, yet the idea of the means was dreadful.

But even in all these moments of distress my health was perfect; and God Almighty never forsook me, as I bore my misfortunes with calmness and resignation. I found all my comfort in religion. We hardly knew anything from out of doors, and were often in fear of the mob breaking into the prison, and renewing the scenes of September—scenes which we could not forget, for the walls of our refectory, and even the wooden chairs, were still stained with the blood and brains of the venerable old priests who had been murdered there on that horrible day!

I forgot to mention that General Santerre —the same who had conducted the unfortunate King to the scaffold, and who had ordered the drums to be beat that his august voice might not be heard by the people—was also a prisoner in the Carmes. He never could live in friendship with me, though he was always attentive. Many of our great ladies were very intimate with him, and thought him a good-natured, harmless man. He assured us all, when we used to abuse him about his conduct on the

21st of January, that he had orders if the King spoke to have all the cannons fired at him, and that it was to avoid that measure he had acted as he did.   He always swore that he regretted the King's death.   This, however, I never believed.   He was liberated before the death of Robespierre, owing, I believe, to his giving our gaoler good beer, for he was a brewer.   He used to send us little trifles for our comfort, and I will say that he never lost an opportunity of serving us.   When he was at liberty he sent me a pound of the finest green tea I ever drank, and some sugar. He also sent us a pie ; but the gaoler liked that too well to give us any of it.

I was very ungrateful to Santerre, as I never saw him but once after I left the prison, and that was in coming out of the Opera.   I was ashamed to be seen speaking to him, though he lived a good deal with some of the ladies who had been in prison, and whom he really had served, in getting them their liberty after the death of Robespierre sooner than they otherwise would have done.

He said that he had never spoken to the

Duke of Orleans in his life till after the King's death. This I readily believe, for the Duke had often declared to me that he never had spoken to Santerre, though he always passed for one of his chief agents.

[Here the manuscript terminates.]

After an imprisonment of full eighteen months in various places, Mrs. Elliott was again restored to liberty. She had been fed during her incarceration upon pickled herrings, at the rate of twopence a-day, with one bottle of water for all purposes. Her captivity was shared, latterly, with Madame Beauharnais, afterwards Madame Bonaparte, and also with a notable person, Madame De Fontenaye, subsequently Madame Tallien. All three, indeed, very narrowly escaped destruction, for they were ordered for execution, and their locks shorn, on the very day that France was delivered by Providence from the monster Robespierre. On emerging from prison she immediately sent for a broker, and disposed of such an amount of her property as enabled her to pay and discharge her establishment of servants, sold her house in Paris to General Murat* (afterwards King of Naples), and took a cottage at Meudon. Here she lived, subsisting on her remaining property, and mixing in the higher circles in Paris during the Consulate and Empire.

By the law of France, after the Revolution, it became necessary for all resident foreigners to adopt a native of the country, to inherit their property. Mrs. Elliott, accordingly, selected the daughter of an English groom in the stables of the Duke of Orleans. This young person, who was educated by her, had a remarkable talent for music; and inherited whatever property Mrs. Elliott possessed at her death.

Of the great man who filled the world with the fame of his conquests, Mrs. Dalrymple Elliott used to relate many anecdotes of the period when he was comparatively little known. She had even received an offer of

* It was afterwards sold to General Lannes, Duc de Montebello.

marriage from him, which, however, she rejected.

On returning to Paris, one day, and paying a visit to Madame Beauharnais, she found her under the hands of the hair-dresser. On the sofa lay a magnificent blue and silver dress. On observing it, Mrs. Elliott, in admiration, exclaimed: "How very charming! And where may you be going in this splendid attire, dear?"

"Oh, stay a few moments," replied Madame Beauharnais, who spoke tolerably good English, "till the hair-dresser is gone, and I will tell you all about it. Look at that dress: it is from your country." She then related to Mrs. Elliott that she had been married that morning to General Bonaparte, at the Municipality, and that he had obtained the command of the army of Italy. She had no affection for him, she said, but Barras had recommended her to accept him. "How could you marry a man with such a horrid name?" said Mrs. Elliott. "Why, I thought," replied Madame Beauharnais, "that he might be of service to my

children.   I am going to dine at the Directory
by-and-by, and shall go a part of the way with
Bonaparte."

Mrs. Elliott saw no more of her until after
Bonaparte became First Consul, when she
went to the Tuileries. The First Consul, it
is known, was fond of children. On this
occasion Madame Bonaparte drew his attention to some beautiful children who were walk-
ing in the gardens of the Tuileries.   He
inquired "who they were?"   "They are the
children of an English gentleman, Mr. Clarke,"
was the reply.

"English!" he exclaimed with bitterness.
"I wish the earth would open and swallow
them up."

"Well, General," remarked Mrs. Elliott,
"that is not very gallant to me."

"Oh!" replied Bonaparte, "I don't consider you to be English—you are a Scotchwoman."

"Ah!" she rejoined, "I am prouder of being
an Englishwoman than of anything."

Bonaparte could not bear to see women with

uncovered shoulders, which was the fashion in Paris at that time. "Make a huge fire," he would say, "I am sure the ladies will perish with cold."

After the conquest of Italy, Barras, who became acquainted with the indiscreet conduct of Madame Bonaparte in her husband's absence, strongly urged her to leave Paris immediately and join him, assuring her that Madame Letitia, the General's mother, (who highly disapproved of the marriage of the First Consul with Madame Beauharnais,) had set out to inform Bonaparte of her intrigue with a young officer. She instantly adopted his advice, and fortunately for her, arrived before the General's mother reached the camp, whose story was thus anticipated and discredited.

At the period of the signing the Treaty of Peace at Amiens, in 1801, Lord Malmesbury, the British Plenipotentiary, met Mrs. Elliott in society, and recommended her to return to England with him. Of this opportunity she availed herself, travelling under the assumed name of Madame St. Maur. For a short time

she resided at Brompton, at the house of a Mrs.
Naylor, where lodgings had been procured for
her, by her direction, by her maid, Madame
La Rue. It was during her residence here,
that, one day when she was out shopping with
Mrs. Naylor, her attention was drawn to a
post-chaise and four by a gentleman thrusting
out his head and regarding her with fixed
attention.   She soon recognised in the traveller
the Hon. Charles Wyndham, brother of Lord
Egremont.   It afterwards appeared that he
was travelling to Brighton to join a party, at
which the Prince of Wales was to be present,
at the Pavilion, then the mansion of the Earl,
and subsequently the property of the Prince.
On his arrival, when the party was assembled,
he piqued their curiosity as to the person he
had encountered on his way, a lady whom
they all knew, and for whom, as we have
seen, the Prince entertained the warmest regard—" Who do you think the lady was?"
said he.   Having raised their curiosity to the
highest pitch, at length he said, " One from
the grave—Mrs. Elliott, even more beautiful

than ever." The Prince was so delighted at the intelligence, that he returned that very night to town, and sent her a most affectionate letter, begging her to go to him. Accordingly, dressed in the simplest manner, she went to Carlton House, and was received with great warmth by the Prince; and their old friendship was renewed.

Mrs. Elliott remained in England until 1814, when the Bourbon family was restored to the throne of France. During the whole period of her residence here, from 1801 to 1814, the lady who has kindly contributed much of the information here collected resided with her, and she also accompanied her to Paris, and remained with her ten weeks. The cruelties and privations which Mrs. Elliott had endured during her iniquitous confinement produced a most injurious and lasting effect on her constitution. She was long an invalid, and for six months was tenderly nursed by the lady here alluded to.

Mrs. Elliott returned to Paris at the same time as the Royal Family of France, to whom

restoration was accompanied with very pain-
ful reminiscences.   It was with bitter feeling
and tears that the poor Duchesse d'Angoulême
regarded this event: hers indeed had been a
life of poignant grief and troubles !   The Duc
de Bourbon was also most unhappy on the
occasion.   In England he said he had lived
tranquilly, and was loth to leave it.   "What
do I go to France for," he said, "but to meet
the murderers of my son?"

Mrs. Elliott had the satisfaction of seeing
the Marquis de Chansenets (whose life she had
saved at so great risk to her own) reinstated as
Governor of the Tuileries.

We have referred to her exquisite beauty.
Mrs. Elliott's daughter, Lady Charles Ben-
tinck, who was always very affectionate to her,
used to say, that on looking round on the
brilliant assemblage of lovely women to be
found in the Opera House of London, she saw
no one comparable to her mother for beauty
and elegance of manners.

The late Duke of Cambridge, on one occasion, passing along the Edgeware Road,

Sir Joshua Reynolds pinx.   J. Brown, sc.

LADY CHARLOTTE BENTINCK.

London, Richard Bentley, 1838

observed the panel of a carriage on which the royal arms were quartered, and inquired into the circumstance. He afterwards went to Carlton House and mentioned what he had learnt; on which the Prince sent an intimation that the quartering of the royal arms would not be permitted, there being no precedent for it since the days of the merry monarch, Charles II.

The chequered life of this greatly-admired and lovely woman quietly terminated at Ville d'Avray. She had witnessed with most intense grief the overthrow of the French monarchy, and the cruel murder of Louis the Sixteenth, but fortunately did not survive (it is believed) to see the fresh troubles of France in 1830, which finally terminated in the expulsion of the elder branch of the Bourbon family.

Thus ended the life of this remarkable woman; at one time cherished by the Princes and nobles of the land—at another, the miserable companion of nobles and peasants, reduced to one common level of wretchedness, expecting one moment to be led away to the scaffold, amidst the yells of an infuriated and brutal mob, and at another to perish from starvation and neglect.

THE END.

LONDON:
PRINTED BY WILLIAM CLOWES AND SONS, STAMFORD STREET
AND CHARING CROSS.

8, New Burlington Street,
December, 1858.

MR. BENTLEY'S
LIST OF NEW WORKS,

NOW READY.

HANS C. ANDERSEN.

To Be or Not to Be.

By Hans Christian Andersen, Author of 'The Improvisatore.'
Crown 8vo. 5*s*.

> "This work is charmingly written."—*Athenæum.*

MISS AUSTEN.

Novels of Miss Austen :

Emma, Sense and Sensibility, Pride and Prejudice,
Mansfield Park, Northanger Abbey, and Persuasion. A
Library Edition, in 5 vols. small 8vo, with Ten Illustrations, 15*s*.

> "Miss Austen has a talent for describing the involvements, and feelings, and characters of ordinary life, which is to me the most wonderful I ever met with. Her exquisite touch, which renders ordinary commonplace things and characters interesting from the truth of the description and the sentiment, is denied to me."—*Sir Walter Scott.*

Anne Sherwood.

A Novel. 3 vols. post 8vo, 10*s*.

> "Written in a style of bold and powerful invective that might have become a female Juvenal. It is a most remarkable novel."—*Press.*
>
> "Its deep, passionate energy, is like Charlotte Bronte's 'Jane Eyre.'"—*John Bull.*

A

GEORGE BANCROFT.

History of the American Revolution.

By GEORGE BANCROFT. 3 vols, 8vo. 31s. 6d.

"This work must take its place as an essentially satisfactory history of the United States. Mr. Bancroft's style is original and national, breathing of the mountain and the prairie. A strain of wild and forest-like music swells up in almost every line. The story is told richly and vividly. In his hands American scenery is full of fine effects. Steeped in the colours of his imagination, a thousand incidents, thought dull before, appear now animated and pictorial. In his narrative all is movement. His men glow with human purposes—his story sweeps on with the exulting life of a procession."—*Athenæum.*

T. HAYNES BAYLY.

The Songs, Ballads, and other Poems

of THOMAS HAYNES BAYLY. Edited by his Widow. Post 8vo, with Portrait, 7s. 6d.

"Haynes Bayly's Songs are dramatic in a high degree. Associations by many tuneful firesides, with images of domestic tenderness and cheerful household enjoyment, they will doubtless rise to the reader's recollection, and be of greater force to recommend this pleasant volume than any praise of ours."—*Examiner.*

CUTHBERT BEDE.

Fairy Fables.

By CUTHBERT BEDE. Square 8vo, with numerous beautiful Illustrations by ALFRED CROWQUILL. Handsomely bound, 4s.

"A pretty volume, full of short, fresh, and fascinating tales for the parlour and nursery fireside."—*Leader.*

"Pleasant tales of the right sort, with some clever pictures by Alfred Crowquill."—*Athenæum.*

CHARLES L. BRACE.

Life in Norway and Sweden.

By CHARLES LORING BRACE, Author of 'Home Life in Germany.' Crown 8vo, with Illustrations, 9s.

"A dashing, spirited book, and a welcome addition to the carpet-bag of all northern travellers."—*Athenæum.*

JAMES BOSWELL.

Letters of James Boswell,

the Biographer of Dr. Johnson, to the Rev. William Temple. 8vo, 14s.

"Equally with the famous biography of Dr. Johnson, these Letters have the charm of sincerity—a charm which, as long as the world lasts, will be the greatest which the writings of one man can have for another. Boswell never disappoints us. He is an unfailing joke. Whether he writes about love, or riches, or literature, he is always the same, inimitable and inexhaustible. It is rarely that we come across a volume with so much to entertain us and make us laugh."—*Saturday Review.*

BENTLEY.

Bentley's Two Shilling Volumes.

IT IS NEVER TOO LATE TO MEND. By CHARLES READE.

THE COURSE OF TRUE LOVE. By CHARLES READE.

ASPEN COURT. By SHIRLEY BROOKS.

CONFESSIONS OF A THUG. By Captain MEADOWS TAYLOR.

THE INITIALS. By the Author of 'Quits.'

THE CARDINAL. By ARCHIBALD BOYD.

NEARER AND DEARER. By CUTHBERT BEDE.

DELHI; THE CITY OF THE GREAT MOGUL. By Mrs. COLIN MAC-KENZIE.

ROUGHING IT IN THE BUSH. By Mrs. MOODIE.

OUR ANTIPODES; OR, RESIDENCE AND RAMBLES IN THE AUSTRALASIAN COLONIES. By General MUNDY.

THE CONQUEST OF CANADA. By Major WARBURTON, R.A.

GHOST STORIES AND PHANTOM FANCIES. By HAIN FRISWELL.

Any of these volumes can also be had, very handsomely bound in blue cloth, 3s.

"Mr. Bentley's far-famed Two Shilling Series."—*John Bull.*

Bentley's Edition of Ainsworth's 'Rookwood.'

With Illustrations, 3s. 6d.

A 2

The Bentley Ballads.

A Selection of the choice Songs, Ballads, etc., contributed to 'Bentley's Miscellany,' including the famous productions of Father Prout and Dr. Maginn.   Edited by Dr. DORAN.   Crown 8vo, with Illustrated Title, 5s.

Bulwer's Three Stories,

EUGENE ARAM, LAST DAYS OF POMPEII, and PAUL CLIFFORD. Bentley's Edition.   3 vols. 12mo, 15s., with Six Illustrations.

SHIRLEY BROOKS.

The Gordian Knot.

By SHIRLEY BROOKS.   8vo, with Twenty-four beautiful Illustrations by TENNIEL.

FRANCIS T. BUCKLAND.

Curiosities of Natural History.

By FRANCIS T. BUCKLAND, M.A., Student of Christ Church, Assistant-Surgeon, 2nd Life-Guards.   Fourth Edition, in small 8vo, with Illustrations, 6s.

REV. R. W. BROWNE.

History of Roman Classical Literature.

By the Rev. R. W. BROWNE, Professor of History at King's College, London.   Second Edition.   8vo, 12s.

" Professor Browne is not only a classical scholar, but one of the most graceful of English modern writers.   In clearness, purity, and elegance of style, his compositions are unsurpassed ; and his sketches of the lives and works of the great authors of antiquity are models of refined taste and sound criticism.   This is a work which for utility of design and excellence of execution may challenge comparison with any which the present century has produced ; nor can we hesitate to regard it as a very valuable instrument for the instruction of the national mind, and the elevation of the national taste."—*Morning Post.*

REV. R. W. BROWNE.

History of Greek Classical Literature.

By the Rev. R. W. BROWNE, Professor of History at King's College, London. 8vo, 12*s.*

"One of those books that will extend the circle of Greek knowledge far beyond the limits which comprise those persons with whom classical studies are a profession. Mr. Browne's short biographies of the various Greek writers, his plots of tragedies and comedies, his well-chosen anecdotes, agreeably diversify his critical and historical disquisitions."—*Times.*

Checkmate.

Post 8vo, 10*s.* 6*d.*

"The moral of this story is that many have religion enough to make them miserable, but not enough to make them happy."—*John Bull.*

W. WILKIE COLLINS.

Rambles beyond Railways;

or, Notes taken afoot in Cornwall. By W. WILKIE COLLINS, Author of 'Antonina,' 'The Dead Secret,' etc. Square 8vo, with beautiful Coloured Lithographs, 10*s.* 6*d.*

"A very pleasant book, in which the most is made of a happily-chosen subject. The author takes us through all the rocky wonders and beauties of the Cornish coast, from St. German's to the Land's End."—*Times.*

PROFESSOR CREASY.

The Fifteen Decisive Battles of the World,

from Marathon to Waterloo. By Professor CREASY. Ninth Edition, with Plans, 8vo, 10*s.* 6*d.*

"It was a happy idea of Professor Creasy to select for military description those few battles of which, in the words of Hallam, 'a contrary event would have essentially varied the drama of the world in all its subsequent scenes.' The decisive features of the battles are well and clearly brought out, the reader's mind is attracted to the world-wide importance of the event he is considering, while their succession carries him over the whole stream of European history."—*Spectator.*

PETER CUNNINGHAM.

Letters of Horace Walpole, Earl of Orford.

Now first Chronologically arranged. With upwards of One Hundred New Letters. Edited by PETER CUNNINGHAM. 9 vols. 8vo, with Thirty-nine exquisite Portraits, £4. 14s. 6d.

"Horace Walpole will be long known to posterity by his incomparable Letters—models as they are of every variety of epistolary excellence. But it is not only for the merits of his style that Walpole's Letters are, we think, destined more surely perhaps than any other work of his or our age, to immortality; it is because these letters are, in fact, a chronicle of every occurrence and of every opinion which attracted or deserved public attention, either at home or abroad, during one of the busiest half centuries of European history. This correspondence is, in fact, a perfect encyclopædia of information from the very best sources—politics from the fountain-head of parties—debates by the best of reporters—foreign affairs from an *habitué* of diplomatic society—sketches of public characters by their intimate acquaintance or associate—the gossip of fashionable life from a man of fashion—literature from a man of letters—the arts from a man of taste—the news of the town from a member of every club in St. James's Street; and all this related by a pen whose vivacity and graphic power is equalled by nothing but the wonderful industry and perseverance with which it was plied through so long a series of years."—*Quarterly Review*.

"Read, if you have not read, all Horace Walpole's Letters, wherever you can find them; the best wit ever published in the shape of letters."—*Sydney Smith*.

"Incomparable Letters."—*Lord Byron*.

"Walpole's great History of his own Times."—*John Wilson Croker*.

"Mr. Cunningham has been entrusted, and his peculiar knowledge justifies the selection, with the editorship of the first collected edition of an English Classic; and as this will no doubt hereafter be the standard one, Cunningham's 'Walpole' will henceforward be as regularly quoted as Tyrwhitt's 'Chaucer.' That Walpole is an English classic, who will gainsay? With the exception of James Howel, he was in point of time the first of English letter-writers. That he is first in literary rank the majority of readers will readily admit. With fancy and imagination enough for a poet, learning sufficient to have established his reputation as a scholar, wit equal to both, and a social position which put him in possession of all the gossip of the day, what wonder is it that Horace Walpole should shine pre-eminent as a letter-writer? His style, modelled upon those sparkling French writers whom he so delighted in, is perfect in its ease; and his pictures of society combine at once the truth of Hogarth and the grace of Watteau. When we add that in his delightful correspondence one may read the political and social history of England from the middle of the reign of George the Second to the breaking out of the first French Revolution, we do not risk damaging our reputation as prophets, when we predict that, great as has been the success of former publications of these Letters, yet greater success will attend the present edition. For be it remembered, this edition contains not only all the letters hitherto published, arranged in chronological order, and many now first collected or first made public, but also the notes of all previous editors, among whom are Lord Dover, Mr. Croker, the Misses Berry, and the Rev. John Mitford. Mr. Cunningham has come to his task, therefore, under very fortunate circumstances. He has been preceded by men familiar with the events and persons of whom Walpole writes, and one less practised in the duties of an editor, less intimate with the literature and history of Walpole's period, than Mr. Cunningham, could scarcely have failed in making a good book; no wonder, then, that with such materials he has produced the work by which he is destined to be remembered hereafter."—*Notes and Queries*.

PROFESSOR CREASY.

Rise and Progress of the English Constitution.

A Popular Account of the Primary Principles, the Formation and Development of the English Constitution, avoiding all Party Politics. By Professor CREASY. Third Edition. Post 8vo, 7*s.* 6*d.*

"An admirable summary of knowledge, which every well-educated Englishman ought to possess."—*Literary Gazette.*

PROFESSOR CREASY.

History of the Ottoman Turks,

from the Foundation of their Empire to the Present Time, chiefly based upon Van Hammer. By Professor CREASY. 1 vol. 8vo, with Maps, 7s. 6d.

"Of all the histories of the Turks this is by far the best."—*Spectator.*

MISS COSTELLO.

Memoirs of Mary, the young Duchess of Bur-

gundy, and her Contemporaries. By LOUISA COSTELLO, Author of 'A Summer among the Bocages and the Vines.' Post 8vo, 10*s.* 6*d.*

SYDNEY DOBELL.

The Roman; a Dramatic Poem.

By SYDNEY DOBELL. Post 8vo, 5*s.*

" We have read this poem with delight. The Author touches with equal power the pathetic and the sublime; he brings a fancy which rivets by its boldness and enchains by its beauty. Should any one, after the extracts we have given, doubt whether we have a new poet amongst us, we should despair of his conversion."—*Athenæum.*

J. D'EWES.

China, Australia, and Islands of the Pacific,

in the Years 1855-56. By J. D'EWES, Esq. Post 8vo, with Illustrations, 10*s.* 6*d.*

" The account of the Chinese and China is by far the most valuable. Mr. J. D'Ewes had good opportunities of seeing the domestic economy of our princely merchants andtheir social relations with the Chinese."—*Spectator.*

DR. DORAN.

Habits and Men,

with Remnants of Records touching the Makers of Both. By Dr. DORAN. Third Thousand. Post 8vo, 7s. 6d.

"As old Burton makes melancholy and its many varieties a canvas whereon he may embroider whatever he thinks fit, so does Dr. Doran take up human attire. Nearly every page contains something amusing; and you may shut the book in the middle and open it again after a twelvemonth's interval, without at all compromising its power of affording enjoyment. We need scarcely add that Dr. Doran's book is not only amusing, but that it is full of strange information that every one would like to possess. Here, in fact, is the note-book of an intelligent, educated, and studious man, enabling the reader, by skimming over pages, to obtain, almost without a thought, an amount of knowledge for which the author has ransacked libraries."—*Times.*

DR. DORAN.

Table Traits and Something on Them.

By Dr. DORAN. Third Edition. Post 8vo, 7s. 6d.

"This entertaining work includes almost everything connected with the pleasures of the table. Dr. Doran exhibits a great amount of reading, very agreeable wit, and a refined scholarship."—*Manchester Times.*

DR. DORAN.

Knights and their Days.

By Dr. DORAN. Second Thousand. Post 8vo, 10s. 6d.

"Satirical, anecdotical, quizzical—full of most wise conceits and ridiculous stories—a book of knights of the stage and knights of the thimble—of mock knights and smock knights—of royal knights and knights of the road,—it is very laughable and very provoking. There is only one word to be said about it—*read it.*"—*Athenæum.*

DR. DORAN.

Monarchs Retired from Business.

By Dr. DORAN. Second Edition, and Second Thousand. 2 vols. post 8vo, 21s. Two Portraits.

"Emphatically a book which will be liked by all classes. With information to recommend it to the studious, its liveliness will attract the desultory reader, and it cannot fail to delight both. It is altogether a very charming book."—*Gentleman's Magazine.*

DR. DORAN.

History of Court Fools.

By Dr. DORAN. Second Thousand. Post 8vo, 10s. 6d.

"Anything more quaint, subtle, and surprising than Dr. Doran's tale of the origin of court fools is scarcely to be found in the pages of the greatest and most genial humourist. Will not many of our readers, on so much acquaintance from our few extracts, desire a still more intimate knowledge of the 'History of Court Fools'?"—*Athenæum.*

DR. DORAN.

Queens of England of the House of Hanover.

By Dr. DORAN. Second Edition, 2 vols. post 8vo, with Illustrations, 21s.

"These 'Lives' indicate afresh the wealth and variety of Dr. Doran's collections."—*Athenæum.*

"An extraordinary repertory of facts and anecdotes."—*Spectator.*

R. H. WALLACE DUNLOP.

The Khakee Ressalah;

Service and Adventure with the Khakee Ressalah, or Meerut Volunteer Horse, during the Mutinies of 1857–8. By ROBERT HENRY WALLACE DUNLOP, B.C.S. Post 8vo, with Coloured Illustrations, 7s. 6d.

"Life-like, real, and bringing before you the everyday life of the resolute body of Irregular Horse, to which Mr. Dunlop owed the carrying out of many a bold attack."—*Morning Advertiser.*

MRS. ELLIS.

Friends at their own Firesides.

By Mrs. ELLIS, Author of 'The Women of England.' 2 vols. fcap. 8vo, 12s.

"The authoress here describes the social and domestic life of the Quakers. Mrs. Ellis, having been herself brought up in a Quaker family, is naturally very fit for such a task, which she executes with all the grace her pen has long been known to possess."—*Statesman.*

B

REV. J. EDWARDS, M.A.

The Andromache of Euripides.

With suggestions and questions at the foot of each page, intended to be read as a first Greek Play. By the Rev. J. EDWARDS, M.A., and the Rev. C. HAWKINS, B.C.L., Ch. Ch. Oxon. Second Edition. Post 8vo, 4s. 6d.

"Every passage of the text is illustrated with an extent of erudition which renders the work of incalculable value to the student."—*Educational Times.*

REV. CHARLES FORSTER.

The One Primeval Language,

Traced experimentally through Ancient Inscriptions in Alphabetical Characters of lost Powers from the four Continents. By the Rev. CHARLES FORSTER, Rector of Stisted. This important work is now published in Three Volumes, demy 8vo, any one Volume of which can be had separately, price 21s. each, or the Three Volumes together, price 42s.

Part I. THE VOICE OF ISRAEL FROM THE ROCKS OF SINAI.

Part II. THE VESTIGES OF PATRIARCHAL TRADITION FROM THE MONUMENTS OF EGYPT, ETRURIA, AND SOUTHERN ARABIA.

Part III. THE MONUMENTS OF ASSYRIA, BABYLONIA, AND PERSIA. WITH A KEY TO THE RECOVERY OF THE LOST TEN TRIBES.

"The work before us lays claim to a great discovery. Mr. Forster has started a theory which deserves the attentive consideration of every Hebrew or Arabic scholar —for if his theory be verified, the result must be an immense accession of light to the whole field of Semitic philology. Mr. Forster thinks that he has already discovered Arabic to be or to contain the one primitive language. The theological value of the records of the miracles of the Exodus graven in the living rocks, by the hands of the very men who witnessed those mighty judgments, is perfectly incalculable."— *Guardian.*

"A very remarkable work. It is one of the most valuable contributions to Scripture evidences we have met with for some time."—*Daily News.*

"It exhibits extensive learning and great philological research; while the author's views, which are altogether novel on the subject, are supported by a mass of extraordinary and highly interesting evidence."—*Critic.*

REV. CHARLES FORSTER.

A Letter to Lord Lyndhurst

in Vindication of the Sinaitic Inscriptions, in Answer to the Rev. Arthur Penrhyn Stanley, M.A. 8vo. 5s.

CHARLES E. FRANCATELLI.

The Modern Cook.

A Practical Guide to the Culinary Art in all its branches. Adapted as well for the Largest Establishments as for the use of Private Families. By CHARLES ELME FRANCATELLI. Fifth Thousand. 8vo. 12s.

> "The destiny of nations depends upon their diet."—*Brillat Savarin.*

> " There's no want of meat, Sir;
> Portly and curious viands are prepared
> To please all kinds of appetites."—*Massinger.*

MARIA FREEMAN.

A Friend in Need.

3 vols. post 8vo. 31s. 6d.

> " A novel full of incident, various in its situations, and abounding with striking and occasionally powerful contrasts—a novel, in fact, equal in point of interest to any recently published."—*Observer.*

> " Certainly deserves to be one of the most popular novels of the season."—*Critic.*

> " A clever, well-constructed romance, abounding in a variety of incidents, powerfully delineated, throughout which the interest of the reader never flags."—*Morning Post.*

FREYTAG.

Debit and Credit.

A Novel. From the German of FREYTAG. Translated by Mrs. MALCOLM. Crown 8vo, 6s.

> "This novel has had an extraordinary circulation in Germany, approaching to that of ' Uncle Tom,' or Mr. Dickens's or Mr. Thackeray's novels in England. Mrs. Malcolm's translation is executed with fidelity and spirit, and with the sanction of the author."—*Times.*

> "The most popular German novel of the age."—*Chevalier Bunsen.*

> "We cannot here give any idea of the variety, vivacity, intensity of this admirable story."—*Statesman.*

Gordon of Duncairn.

2 vols. small 8vo, 12s.

"The tone of the work and the sketches of character exhibit observation and a touch of character. There is a good deal of youthful freshness and the germ of power."—*Spectator.*

"The heroine, Minnie Gray, is one of the sweetest female creations in English literature, and with her companion, Lily Græme, presents a picture of female friendship and confidence most exquisitely drawn and coloured. The moral of the story is excellent, and the catastrophe is brought about with consummate skill."—*Illustrated News of the World.*

CAPTAIN GIBNEY.

My Escape from the Mutinies in Oudh.

By Captain GIBNEY.   2 vols. small 8vo, with Illustrations, 12s.

"Nearly everything, from the first to the last chapter, is true, I can safely state; but all did not occur to myself. Many of the miseries were experienced by other officers somewhat similarly situated. This work was composed partly whilst under a leaky shed on picket duty, watching the arid plains of Rohilcund, at that time given up to murder, pillage, and the wildest confusion; and it was finished on my return to England, sick and wounded, the result of an action with the mutineers."—*Extract from Author's Preface.*

LIEUT.-COL. GRAHAM.

History of the Art of War.

Elementary History of the Progress of the Art of War.   By Lieut.-Col. J. J. GRAHAM.   Post 8vo, with Plans of Battles, 7s. 6d.

"A brief account of the composition of armies—the progress of the art of war from the earliest ages—maxims of modern military science, and a chronology of military events, illustrated by sketches, and the opinions of Frederick the Great, Napoleon, Cæsar, Gustavus, Turenne, Marlborough, and other great commanders, besides Jomini."—*Athenæum.*

MRS. GREEN.

Letters of Queen Henrietta Maria;

Including her Private Correspondence with Charles I.   Edited by MARY ANN EVERETT GREEN.   Post 8vo, 10s. 6d.

"On the history of the Civil War in the seventeenth century, these letters throw important light."—*Literary Gazette.*

EARL GREY.

An Essay on Parliamentary Reform.

By EARL GREY. 8vo, 7s. 6d.

M. R. GUBBINS.

The Mutinies in Oudh;

An Account of the Mutinies in Oudh and of the Siege of Lucknow Residency; with some observations on the Causes of the Mutiny. By MARTIN RICHARD GUBBINS, Financial Commissioner for Oudh. Third Edition. One vol. 8vo, with Maps and Illustrations.

"This book will probably soon supersede all others as a record of the revolt of Oudh, mainly because it combines with a clear, circumstantial, and simple narrative of the events of the memorable siege of Lucknow, and with beautifully-coloured illustrations of the localities, a masterly and dispassionate survey of the state of Oudh before the siege, and of the various causes to which the revolt of the province has been attributed."—*Economist*.

"The second edition is enriched by two notable narratives—a lady's escape from Sultanpore, and Major Eyre's account of the famous Arrah expedition. This is the most important book on the siege of Lucknow yet published, or ever likely to be published."—*Examiner*.

ARNOLD GUYOT.

Lectures on Physical Geography;

Or, Earth and Man. By ARNOLD GUYOT. The only unabridged edition. Small 8vo, 2s. 6d.

"We have never seen the science of physical geography explained with greater clearness and elegance."—*Athenæum*.

M. GUIZOT.

Memoirs of my Own Time.

By M. GUIZOT. Vols. I. and II., in 8vo, 14s. each.

"Will be devoured as a history of our own times by one of the most conspicuous men now alive, and will be referred to hereafter when much popular literature will have been devoured by the worms. Guizot is a man of genius—and genius is immortality. This is one of the few books that will mark the generation that gives it birth." —*Athenæum*.

C

M. GUIZOT.

Memoirs of Sir Robert Peel.

By M. GUIZOT. 8vo. 14s.

"The most impartial estimate of Sir Robert Peel we have seen."—*Athenæum.*

M. GUIZOT.

History of Charles the First

and the English Revolution. By M. GUIZOT. 2 vols. 8vo, 28s.

"The best history, both in thought and composition, of the Reign of Charles the First."—*Edinburgh Review.*

M. GUIZOT.

History of Oliver Cromwell

and the English Commonwealth. By M. GUIZOT. 2 vols. 8vo, 28s.

"M. Guizot has given us an admirable narrative, far more candid than any from an English pen."—*Times.*

"M. Guizot has unravelled Cromwell's character with singular skill. No one, in our opinion, has drawn his portrait with equal truth. M. Guizot's acquaintance with our annals, language, customs, and politics, is altogether extraordinary. He is an earnest and profound writer."—*Quarterly Review.*

M. GUIZOT.

History of Richard Cromwell

and the Dawn of the Restoration. By M. GUIZOT. 2 vols. 8vo, 28s.

"It is impossible to read this calm and noble work without feeling its unconscious pathos. M. Guizot here shows us the last act of a great drama, terrible in its interest and tragic at the close."—*Athenæum.*

"M. Guizot's narrative is masterly. Perhaps no period of equal importance could be less attractive as the subject of a history; yet these volumes are more interesting than most descriptions of brilliant and exciting times. The execution of the translation is excellent; M. Guizot has had ample justice done to the spirited and balanced language in which his thoughts are expressed. Generally the thoughts to which M. Guizot gives a distinct shape are profound and just; he especially excels in those statements—half fact, half reflection—in which the whole position and aim of a party is described and commented on."—*Saturday Review.*

M. GUIZOT.

Corneille and his Times.

By M. GUIZOT. 8vo, 10s. 6d.

———◆———

M. GUIZOT.

Shakespeare and his Times.

By M. GUIZOT. 8vo, 10s. 6d.

———◆———

JAMES HAMILTON.

Sinai, the Hedjaz, and Soudan :

Wanderings round the Birthplace of the Prophet, and across the Ethiopian Desert, with Pictures of Arab Life. By JAMES HAMILTON, Author of 'Wanderings in Northern Africa.' Post 8vo, 10s. 6d. Maps.

"A work of great importance—a valuable contribution to the history and geography of a region associated with our earliest studies, and for the classical scholar invested by the oldest Greek historian with never-fading charms."—*Standard.*

———◆———

THOMAS INGOLDSBY.

The Ingoldsby Legends ;

Or, Mirth and Marvels. 3 vols. post 8vo, with all the Illustrations of GEORGE CRUIKSHANK and JOHN LEECH. 21s.

The same work in One Volume, small 8vo, with Illustrated Frontispiece, 5s. This Five Shilling Edition contains the whole of the Legends, the Life of Thomas Ingoldsby alone being omitted.

"Abundant in humour, observation, fancy; in extensive knowledge of books and men; in palpable hints of characters, exquisitive grave irony, and the most whimsical indulgences of point and epigram : we doubt if even Butler beats the author of these 'Legends' in the easy drollery of verse. We cannot open a page that is not sparkling with its wit and humour—that is not ringing with its strokes of pleasantry and satire."—*Examiner.*

WILLIAM JAMES.

James's Naval History of Great Britain,

with a Continuation to the Battle of Navarino. By Captain CHAMIER. Embellished with 23 beautiful Portraits of the most distinguished Officers engaged in the late eventful War. 6 vols. demy 8vo, 42s.

"This book is one of which it is not too high praise to assert, that it approaches as nearly to perfection, in its own line, as any historical work perhaps ever did. The principal transactions narrated in it, and we trust by this time the narrative itself, are fortunately too well known to require a detailed notice of its contents. But a general sketch of its plan, and the manner of its execution, will, we think, convince our readers that the high character we have given of it is not exaggerated. Mr. James commences his work with a very useful Introduction, in which he briefly and clearly sketches the progress of Naval Architecture in Great Britain, and the origin of the principal improvements in the British Navy before the time of the French Revolution. The history itself opens with the declaration of war in 1793, and closes with the general peace of 1815.* Every year between these two periods occupies a separate division of the work; and every such division is subdivided under three heads, detailing respectively the movements of the hostile fleets, the encounters of single ships and boat attacks, and all colonial naval operations. The research necessary to procure materials for twenty-eight such abstracts, and the labour of composing them, must have been so great that they alone may be considered as a striking monument of industry. With a candour almost as uncommon as his accuracy, he never fails to notice any variation of consequence in the statements of the hostile party; and either to refute it by argument, or fairly to balance it with the opposing testimony. We cannot contemplate without admiration the impartial and unwearied zeal for historical truth, which alone could have supported him through his tedious and thankless labours."—*Edinburgh Review.*

* Since brought down to the Battle of Navarino.

---◆---

J. W. KAYE.

Memorials of Indian Government.

By HENRY ST. GEORGE TUCKER. Edited by JOHN WILLIAM KAYE. 8vo, 16s.

---◆---

J. W. KAYE.

The Life of Henry St. George Tucker,

late Accountant-General of Bengal, and Chairman of the Hon. East India Company. By JOHN WILLIAM KAYE. 8vo, 16s. Portrait.

J. W. KAYE.

History of the War in Afghanistan.

By JOHN WILLIAM KAYE. 3 vols. 12mo, 15s.

"This vivid narrative is written with scrupulous and unflinching fidelity, whilst even the best-known details acquire the freshness of novelty from the skill displayed in weaving them into a narrative. Mr. Kaye's laborious researches seem to have been guided by a love of truth powerful enough to divest his mind of all personal partialities. The Afghan war is now presented to us with an approach to dramatic unity of form and purpose, the development of the plot subserving to the legitimate end of all dramatic composition—the enforcement of a great moral truth."—*Quarterly Review.*

MISS KAVANAGH.

Madeline; a Tale of Auvergne.

By JULIA KAVANAGH, Author of 'Nathalie.' Second Edition. Small 8vo, Illustration, 3s. 6d.

"One of those rare books which at once touch the feelings by a simple and forcible truthfulness to nature. It is destined to permanent popularity, and the name of the writer will be marked with those of Madame Cottin and St. Pierre."—*Atlas.*

R. B. KIDD.

The Primary Principles of Reasoning.

A Delineation of the Primary Principles of Reasoning. By ROBERT BOYD KIDD, B.A., Perpetual Curate of Botley, Suffolk. Post 8vo, 9s. 6d.

"I know the most eminent logicians existing, and I do not know Mr. Kidd's superior."—*Archbishop Whately.*

COLONEL LAKE.

The Defence of Kars.

Historical and Military Narrative of the Defence of Kars. By Colonel ATWELL LAKE, C.B. With numerous Lithographic Illustrations. 8vo. 15s.

"This work is a military study, and should become a class-book."—*Leader.*

COLONEL LAKE.

The Story of our Captivity.

Story of our Captivity in Russia. By Colonel ATWELL LAKE, C.B. Post 8vo, 3s. 6d.

M. DE LAMARTINE.

Memoirs of Remarkable Characters.

By ALPHONSE DE LAMARTINE. New Edition, 3 vols. crown 8vo, 15s.

"This work will materially raise the reputation of Lamartine. Along with the brilliancy of style and warmth of imagination which characterize all his writings, we find here gravity of thought and earnestness of purpose. The subject also is well suited to his peculiar genius and talents. As a sketcher of historical scenes and of historical characters, choosing his own subjects, suggested by his own tastes or sympathies, no living author is capable of greater or more successful efforts. In these volumes we have a gallery of illustrious portraits, drawn in bold and striking style, and glowing with life-like feeling and expression. The translation of the work has been prepared with care, and in several cases historical inaccuracies are pointed out and corrected."—*Literary Gazette.*

DR. LEE.

The Last Days of the Emperor Alexander

and the First Days of the Emperor Nicholas. By ROBERT LEE, M.D. Small 8vo, 3s. 6d.

The Ladies of Bever Hollow.

By the Author of 'Mary Powell,' etc. New Edition, small 8vo, 5s.

"This is a thoroughly English story. The incidents are slight, and not exciting; but the characters are well drawn, and the conversations being full of life and spirit, the interest never for a moment flags. The author of 'Mary Powell' has in this picture of country life proved herself a literary Gainsborough."—*Athenæum.*

"Simple and quiet is the new tale by the authoress of 'Mary Powell.' It is a half old-fashioned, half new-fashioned, tale of country life, and country love, and country gossipings."—*Examiner.*

M'CAUSLAND.

Sermons in Stones;

or, Scripture confirmed by Geology. By D. M'CAUSLAND. Sixth Edition, small 8vo, with Nineteen Illustrations, 4s.

The object of the author in this work is to prove that the Mosaic narrative of the Creation is reconcilable with the established facts of geology; and that geology not only establishes the truth of the first page of the Bible, but that it furnishes the most direct and sensible evidence of the fact of Divine inspiration, and thereby authenticates the whole canon of Scripture. The word of God is thus authenticated by His works.

LIEUT. MARTELLI, R.N.

Naval Officer's Guide

for Preparing Ships for Sea. By Lieut. CHARLES MARTELLI, R.N.
Fcap. 8vo, 6s.

"A masterly exposition of those complex details on which the efficiency of our ships depends."—*United Service Journal.*

GENERAL MARKHAM.

Shooting Scenes in the Himalayas,

Chinese Tartary, Ladak, Thibet, etc. By the late GENERAL MARK-
HAM, 91st Regiment. Imperial 8vo, with Lithographic Illustrations, 21s.

"These sporting adventures in the loftiest region of the globe are rapid, readable, varied, interesting, and never tedious from overdoing. The introduction of rare animals is accompanied by an account of them, and the narrative is relieved by pic-tures of the sublime scenery among which the pursuit led, as well as by anecdotes and sketches of the people. The character of the Colonel is well adapted to the style of the sportsman: frank, genial, and with fine spirits, he has also a wide knowledge of men and sporting."—*Spectator.*

LORD MAHON.

Letters and Works of Philip Dormer Stanhope,

Earl of Chesterfield. Including numerous Letters and Sketches
hitherto unpublished. Now first collected. By Lord MAHON
(Earl Stanhope). Five vols., 8vo, with Portrait, 56s.

"Of these famous letters it cannot be said that until now they had received even a decent measure of editorial care. Lord Mahon has reproduced them entire, and for the first time filled up names left in blank, and explained hints and allusions which the lapse of another generation would have condemned to hopeless obscurity. When we compare Lord Mahon's copy with what we had had before, it is hardly too much to say that he has given us a new work. Whatever could wound anybody's feelings had been omitted; in other words, a very large proportion of whatever could throw light on the secret history of parties and public men in Lord Chesterfield's time—very many letters entirely—the most striking paragraphs of half the rest. The *lacunæ* are now filled up as far as was possible, and the whole illustrated by notes brief and clear."—*Quarterly Review.*

MRS. COLIN MACKENZIE.

The Great Day of Atonement ;

or, Meditations and Prayers on the last Twenty-four Hours of the Sufferings and Death of our Lord and Saviour Jesus Christ. Translated from the German of CHARLOTTE ELIZABETH NEBELIN. Edited by Mrs. COLIN MACKENZIE, Author of 'The Mission, the Camp, and the Zenana,' etc.   Post 8vo, 2*s.* 6*d.*

This work was written by the daughter of the honoured Pastor Rambach, about the middle of the last century, and was revised by the venerable Pastor Köllner, who, being in his 75th year, thanked God that he had been permitted to finish this revision.

THE EARL OF MALMESBURY.

Diary of the Earl of Malmesbury.

The Diaries and Correspondence of the Earl of Malmesbury. Edited by his Grandson, the present Earl.   4 vols. 8vo, 42*s.* Portraits.

"This mode of anticipating history has great charms.   How much more delightful to us must be the sketches of George III. and George IV.—Queen Charlotte and Queen Caroline—Pitt and Fox—Canning and Windham (to say nothing of minor portraits)—all fresh, as it were, from the hand of a painter, their contemporary, and in some degree ours—than they will be in another generation.   No extracts that our space would allow us to make could afford an adequate idea of the great mass of mingled gossip and history to be found in these volumes.   To us nothing can be more attractive; we seem to be living our youth over again."—*Quarterly Review.*

REV. J. B. MARSDEN.

Dictionary of Christian Churches and Sects,

from the Earliest Ages of Christianity.   By the Rev. J. B. MARSDEN, Incumbent of St. Peter's, Birmingham, Author of "The History of the Early and Later Puritans," etc.   New Edition, in one handsome Volume.   8vo, 12*s.*

"Mr. Marsden's information is well digested, his judgment sound and impartial, his manner of statement not only clear, but with a sustained vividness.   The work has somewhat the appearance of an Encyclopædia, but it is only in appearance.   The exposition has the freshness of an original work.   The philosophic impartiality of the author should not be passed over.   He has, of course, opinions, but he indulges in no violence or harshness of censure.   The arrangement is well adapted for the important point of conveying complete and full information."—*Spectator.*

A Timely Retreat from Meerut.

By Two SISTERS. Second Edition. 2 vols. post 8vo. Illustrations, 21s.

"We have not had such a picture of Anglo-Indian daily life since the late Miss Roberts published her experiences. But these two volumes have an additional interest; it was a plucky undertaking, and the narrative is told with animation and truthfulness."—*Spectator.*

Notes on Noses.

Hints towards a Classification of Noses. With numerous Illustrations. 2s.

"Worthy of Lawrence Sterne."—*Morning Post.*

₄ 6000 copies of this little book have been sold.

SIR CHARLES NAPIER.

The History of the Baltic Campaign of 1854.

From Documents and other Materials furnished by Vice-Admiral Sir CHARLES NAPIER, K.C.B. Edited by G. BUTLER EARP. 8vo, 16s.

Philip Paternoster.

A Tractarian Love Story. 2 vols. small 8vo, 12s.

"A smart and slashing production, written with the intention of exterminating Puseyism, by making every Puseyite thoroughly ashamed of himself."—*Morning Star.*

REV. HENRY POLEHAMPTON.

Polehampton Letters and Diaries.

A Memoir, Letters, and Diary of the late Rev. Henry S. Pole-hampton, Fellow of Pembroke College, Oxford, Chaplain of Luck-now. The Diary extends to July 18, 1857, two days before his death in the Residency, from which date it is continued by his Widow. Edited by the Rev. EDWARD POLEHAMPTON, M.A., and the Rev. THOMAS STEDMAN POLEHAMPTON, M.A., Fellows of Pembroke College, Oxford. Second Edition, in post 8vo, with Illustrations, 10s. 6d.

"This book is one which needs no praise : it is of no pretence, offering simply a loving account of a good man's life, closed amid circumstances that made it heroic."
—*Athenæum.*

"The name of the brave, overworked Chaplain who died in the siege of Lucknow, and the noble devotion of his widow to the sick and wounded, are well known where-ever there are Englishmen to read the story of the Indian war. The inventions of the novelist are good indeed if they are not surpassed in interest by records like these."—*Examiner.*

Quits.

By the Author of 'The Initials.' 3 vols. post 8vo, 15s.

"Witty, sententious, graphic, full of brilliant pictures of life and manners, it is positively one of the best of modern stories, and may be read with delightful interest from cover to cover."—*Morning Post.*

Quinland ; or, Varieties in American Life.

2 vols. post 8vo, 7s. 6d.

"Here we have every variety of American life ; life in a clearing, life in an Ameri-can village, and the fashionable life of large towns. We have farmers, storekeepers, and gentlemen ; physicians, lawyers, and alchemists ; hunters, horse-stealers, and usurers ; roguish misers in council with keen attorneys ; and ambitious senators bribing unscrupulous journalists."—*Press.*

CHARLES READE.

It is Never too Late to Mend.

By CHARLES READE. Crown 8vo, 5s. edition, with Illustrations. Also square 8vo, 2s. Edition.

"Written with amazing spirit."—*Press.*

₊ The sale of this work in all forms has reached 57,000 copies.

Rita: an Autobiography.

2 vols. post 8vo, 21s.

"The writing in this book sometimes attains the difficult virtue of a strong simplicity. Here and there the observation of character is singularly acute."—*Literary Gazette.*

"Let readers take up the quiet, gentle, sensible 'Rita;' she will tell them a story of no wonderful incidents, but she will be found narrating the details of a life wherein are the essentials of a novel."—*Athenæum.*

"Neatness of style, pointedness of expression, and cleverness of remark are observable in almost every page. The book is nowhere dull, everywhere displays great freshness, and much vigour of style and power of observation."—*Press.*

MRS. ROMER.

Filia Dolorosa.

Memoirs of the Last Dauphine. By Mrs. ROMER. Second Edition, crown 8vo, 12s. Portrait.

"Exquisitely told."—*Daily News.*

"A more touching picture was never presented to the mind."—*Literary Gazette.*

LORD JOHN RUSSELL.

Memorials and Correspondence of Charles

James Fox. By the Right Hon. Lord JOHN RUSSELL, M.P. 4 vols. 8vo, 56s.

"No Englishman who desires to understand the history of his country from 1768 to 1807 can fail to read this work with advantage and pleasure."—*Edinburgh Review.*

The Ruling Passion.

Three vols., post 8vo, 15s.

"The plot of 'The Ruling Passion' is original, the characters well sketched, and the style good. It is beyond all question a novel of a high order."—*John Bull.*

Salad for the Social.

By the Author of 'Salad for the Solitary.'   Post 8vo, 10s. 6d.

"The essence of a library, the information of a lifetime."—*Morning Chronicle*.

LADY SCOTT.

Types and Antitypes

of the Old and New Testament.   By the Hon. LADY SCOTT.
Post 8vo, 5s. 6d.

"It is but justice to the author of the present volume to state that she has, on the whole, acquitted herself with much ability and sound judgment. Her book will be useful to the class of readers for whom it is principally intended, the young and the comparatively ignorant and uninstructed."—*John Bull.*

REV. W. S. SYMONDS, F.G.S.

Stones of the Valley.

By the Rev. W. S. SYMONDS, F.G.S., Rector of Pendock, Author of 'Old Stones,' and President of the Malvern Natural History Field Club. Foolscap 8vo, 5s.

"Notwithstanding Mr. Symonds's eminent position as a geologist, he has never lost sight of that simplicity in conveying instruction which renders his work admirably suited for the earliest students."—*John Bull.*

M. SIMON.

Natural Religion.

By JULES SIMON.   Translated by J. W. COLE.   Post 8vo, 6s.

"In France, this work has passed through three large editions. It is, indeed, a masterly performance, written with uncommon force and beauty."—*Press.*

"The brevity and force of the reasoning, and the singular aptness of illustration which abound in it, remind one of the most striking passages in Pascal."—*John Bull.*

GEORGE AUGUSTUS SALA.

A Journey Due North;

and Street Life in St. Petersburg. By GEORGE AUGUSTUS SALA, Author of "Twice Round the Clock," etc. Crown 8vo, 5*s.*

" Mr. Sala's pictures of St. Petersburg are vivid and effective beyond those of most travellers. We never remember to have seen before so complete a description of the Gostinnoidvor, or general bazaar, so universal in the Russian towns. The The droschky-driver of St. Petersburg is portrayed with the literal truth and heightened effect of a coloured daguerreotype."—*Times.*

" Lively, witty, entertaining, smartly graphic in description, intensely 'funny.' The book will find many readers who will peruse its pages with pleasure and amusement, not unmixed with information."—*Literary Gazette.*

" Mr. Sala is an admirable companion, full of fun and humour. He dashes off Due North in high glee, and keeps his companion all alive with racy sketches from the beginning to the end of the journey."—*Sunday Times.*

" Mr. Sala is a gentleman not only of quaint wit but of considerable intellectual power. His descriptions of Russian hotels, Russian villages, etc., are all well done." —*Press.*

MISS TILT.

The Old Palace.

By JULIA TILT, Author of 'May Hamilton.' 2 vols. post 8vo, 21*s.*

"The mystery of this story is resolved in an ending of considerable power."— *Spectator.*

M. THIERS.

History of the French Revolution.

By M. THIERS. 5 vols. crown 8vo, with 41 Illustrations. 25*s.*

Illustrations which accompany this Work.

VOL. I.—1. Attack on the Bastille.—2. Portrait of the Duke of Orleans (Égalité).—3. Portrait of Mirabeau.—4. Portrait of Lafayette.—5. Orgies of the Gardes du Corps.—6. Portrait of Marie Antoinette.—7. Return of the Royal Family from Varennes.— 8. Portrait of Marat.—9. The Mob at the Tuileries.—10. Attack on the Tuileries.

VOL. II.—11. Murder of the Princess de Lamballe.—12. Portrait of the Princess de Lamballe.—13. Portrait of Madame Roland.—

14, Louis XVI. at the Convention.—15. Last Interview of Louis XVI. with his Family.—16. Portrait of Louis XVI.—17. Portrait of Dumouriez.—18. Triumph of Marat.—19. Portrait of Laroche-Jacquelin.

Vol. III.—20. Assassination of Marat.—21. Portrait of Charlotte Corday.—22. Portrait of Camille-Desmoulins.—23. Condemnation of Marie Antoinette.—24. Portrait of Bailly (Mayor of Paris).—25. Trial of Danton, Camille-Desmoulins, etc.—26. Portrait of Danton.—27. Portrait of Madame Elisabeth.—28. Carrier at Nantes.—29. Portrait of Robespierre.

Vol. IV.—30. Last Victims of the Reign of Terror.—31. Portrait of Charette.—32. Death of the Deputy Feraud.—33. Death of Romme, Goujon, Duquesnoi, etc.—34. Portrait of Louis XVII.—35. The 13th Vendémiaire (5th October, 1795).

Vol. V.—36. Summoning to Execution.—37. Portrait of Pichegru.—38. Portrait of Moreau.—39. Portrait of Hoche.—40. Portrait of Napoleon Bonaparte.—41. The 18th Brumaire (10th November, 1799).

"The palm of excellence, after whole libraries have been written on the French Revolution, has been assigned to the dissimilar histories of Thiers and Mignet."—*William H. Prescott.*

"I am reading Thiers's French Revolution, which I find it difficult to lay down."—*Rev. Sydney Smith.*

MRS. WEBB.

The Martyrs of Carthage.

By Mrs. WEBB, Author of 'Naomi.'   Second Edition. Fcap. 8vo, with Two Illustrations, 5s.

"A deeply interesting and most ably-written work."—*Morning Herald.*

MRS. WEBB.

Idaline.

A Tale of the Egyptian Bondage. By Mrs. WEBB, Author of 'Naomi.' Fcap. 8vo, with Illustration, 5s.

"A tone of earnestness and piety pervades this narrative."—*Morning Herald.*

ANTHONY TROLLOPE.

The Three Clerks.

By ANTHONY TROLLOPE. 3 vols. post 8vo, 10s. 6d.; also, post 8vo, 2s. 6d.

"Mr. Trollope amply bears out in this work the reputation he acquired by 'Barchester Towers.' There is a great field for amusing description in the varieties of London life brought before us through the various characters of Mr. Trollope's story. We regard the tenderness and self-sacrifice of Linda one of the most graceful and touching pictures of feminine heroism in the whole range of modern novels. We do not know any living writer who draws the portraiture of women more delicately or faithfully than Mr. Trollope."—*John Bull.*

"Here are scenes from family life, more true, more pathetic, and more skilfully sustained than any that can be found, except in the writings of family novelists."—*Saturday Review.*

A. WILLS.

Wanderings among the High Alps.

By ALFRED WILLS. Small 8vo, 7s. 6d. New Edition.

"The new edition of Mr. Wills's 'Wanderings' is a welcome book, not only for its agreeable home-reading as a description of scenery, and a narrative of adventures bravely undertaken and well sustained; but for its use as a stimulator to healthy exertion in a somewhat languid age, and as a companion-guide to those who may follow in the writer's footsteps. The form of the new edition is handy, and more fitted for a pocket companion than the original edition, with sketch-maps that save the trouble of reference. There is also additional matter, including a new chapter on the ascent of Mont Blanc."—*Spectator.*

DR. WHATELY.

Mental Culture

Required for Christian Ministers. By RICHARD WHATELY, Archbishop of Dublin. 8vo, 1s.

DR. WHATELY.

Selections from Writings of Richard Whately,

Archbishop of Dublin. Fcap. 8vo, 5s., or bound in calf, 8s. 6d.

"This volume contains the pith, the cream, the choice bits of Archbishop Whately's writings. One of his great charms is his style, as clear as that of Cobbett and Paley."—*Athenæum.*

CHRISTOPHER WINTER.

Six Months in British Burmah;

or, Inia beyond the Ganges in 1857–58. By CHRISTOPHER WINTER. Post 8vo, with Illustrations, 10s. 6d.

"Instead of a diffuse narrative, Mr. Winter has compressed his notes of a six months' residence in British Burmah into a manual form. His personal adventures occupy comparatively few pages, followed by a series of chapters on the administration, inhabitants, birds, beasts, reptiles, products, climate, language, religion, and history of the province. The volume has its characteristic merit, as being a neat and comprehensive description of a very interesting country not yet exhausted by the enthusiasm of travellers."—*Athenæum.*

C. D. YONGE.

Latin and English Dictionary.

A New Phraseological English-Latin and Latin-English Dictionary By C. D. YONGE.

    Part I.   English-Latin, 9s. 6d.
    Part II. Latin-English, 7s. 6d.

Or the whole work complete in One Volume, strongly bound in roan, 15s.

It was suggested to Mr. Yonge, some years ago, to undertake this work. It has been submitted to the most eminent scholars and masters of schools in the kingdom (Dr. Goodford, Head Master of Eton; Dr. Moberly, of Winchester; Dr. Vaughan, of Harrow; Dr. Goulburn, of Rugby; and Dr. Jelf, of King's College, London), who all agree that a careful examination of Mr. Yonge's Dictionary has convinced them that it would fully supply the want so greatly felt.

They have, in consequence, authorized the book to be described as published "For the use of Eton, Winchester, Harrow, and Rugby Schools, and King's College, London," and ordered that it shall be, for the future, the only English-Latin dictionary used in those, the principal places of education in the kingdom.

"A very capital book, either for the somewhat advanced pupil, the student who aims at acquiring an idiomatic Latin style, or the adult with a knowledge of the language. It is the best—we were going to say the only really useful—Anglo-Latin Dictionary we ever met with."—*Spectator.*

JOHN EDWARD TAYLOR, PRINTER, LITTLE QUEEN STREET, LINCOLN'S INN FIELDS.

Lightning Source UK Ltd.
Milton Keynes UK
UKOW07f1911240615

254078UK00008B/168/P